Overcoming Financial Trauma

Overcoming Financial Trauma

How to Break Free from Guilt, Build Wealth, and Redefine Success

Rahkim Sabree

WILEY

Library of Congress Cataloging-in-Publication Data is Available:

ISBN 9781394341245 (Cloth)
ISBN 9781394341252 (ePub)
ISBN 9781394341269 (ePDF)

Cover Design: Wiley
Cover Image: © Tast Nawarat/Getty Images
Author Photo: Courtesy of the Author
SKY10127251_092525

This book is dedicated to my dad, Iman Karim Sabree, who reminded me throughout the creation of this book that I have been writing this book my whole life and that I've forgotten more than some people will ever know.

Contents

Foreword   ix
Preface   xi

Part I: Exposure — Introducing Financial Trauma   1

Chapter 1: Unpacking Generational and Genetic Financial Trauma   3

Chapter 2: Vicarious Trauma and Financial Fear Through Observation   15

Chapter 3: The Trauma of Poverty and Financial Instability   25

Chapter 4: Human Capital, Human Cost: Workplace and Employment Trauma   33

Chapter 5: Institutional and Systemic Financial Trauma   45

Chapter 6: Family, Societal, and Religious Expectations   53

Part II: Education — Exploring Contextual Frameworks and Methods   71

Chapter 7: How Financial Trauma Manifests in the Mind and Body   73

Chapter 8: Understanding Financial Avoidance and Shame   85

Chapter 9: Financial Literacy as an Intervention Method   97

Chapter 10: Banking and Financial Services   107

Chapter 11: Budgeting, Saving, and Financial Planning with a Healing Mindset   119

Part III: Execution — Implementing Strategies for Financial Healing   125

Chapter 12: Rewriting Your Financial Narrative   127

Chapter 13: Setting Financial Boundaries   139

Chapter 14: Building a Financial Support System   151

Chapter 15: Financial Therapy and Alternative Healing   163

Chapter 16: How to Build a Financial Wellness Program   179

Chapter 17: Philanthropy and Social Responsibility   189

References   197

Acknowledgments   199

About the Author   201

Index   203

Foreword

Rahkim is one of the most authentic, genuine, and articulate people I've had the pleasure to connect with in the last decade. I first came across a tweet he made a couple years ago about business that resonated with me. I offered some unsolicited advice that led to us connecting on Zoom a few weeks later. From there, we've connected almost weekly in some form or another, mainly sharing "podcasts" in the form of extended voice notes via text.

While Rahkim may view me as a "Friendtor," his thought leadership in the area of financial trauma is something I really admire and respect, which is why I believe there is no one better to write this book. Oftentimes, the topic of money is relegated to the quantitative aspects of finance. While it is an important aspect, I think the qualitative and emotional drivers of money, which include culture and personal psychology, often get overlooked and are some of the most important connection points driving people's financial behaviors. This is where Rahkim excels. In this book, he brings clarity and depth to these areas, creating some paradigm shifting perspectives for readers.

While Rahkim is qualified to write this book solely based on the credentials and accolades that he has accumulated in his career, its true impact will come from the multitude of experiences and perspectives that Rahkim infuses in his writing bridging race, money, neuroscience, and identity that provide nuance, cultural context, texture, and depth to make people think deeper.

My mission to decrease the wealth gap by $100 billion and empower people to own their financial agency is a shared core value seen in Rahkim's work, so I am honored to march alongside him as he helps further the mission in his own respective way.

Over the past few years, I have seen Rahkim grow and evolve as a man, entrepreneur, writer, and thought leader, and I know that writing this book, at this time, is exactly what the world needs. It cuts through the noise of the status quo insights and dialogue around money and really unlocks what drives people's decision-making around money.

—George Acheampong

Preface

How (and Why) to Read This Book

(Do Not Skip)

This book is going to focus almost entirely on the phenomenon known as *financial trauma*. I've encountered financial trauma on several fronts that I'll explain throughout this book. Like many, I didn't have the vocabulary to describe what it was I had experienced or was experiencing until I made connections between some texts I was reading during the writing of my book *Financially Irresponsible* around generational trauma and financial behavior. At that point it became clear to me that financial behavior can be attached to a larger issue most won't discuss because it forces an acknowledgment of topics that are traditionally not considered safe for exploration in the conservative audiences that finance broadly, and financial services specifically, tend to be associated with: old, rich white men. At the time I thought—mistakenly—that I created a new term and used it as such. The response from the audiences I engaged with was and continues to be one of curiosity, shock, and amazement as dots are connected in their minds based on my gifting them with new vocabulary. The truth, however, was that financial trauma had been used before me. It has been used largely in academic and clinical circles to describe the "flashpoint" financial experiences due to prolonged financial anxiety or stress, or a major life change. Locked up behind the walls of academia, it left poor and marginalized communities to fend for themselves, however, wrestling with guilt, shame, and self-doubt as they were told that their issues financially only demanded that they become smarter, work harder, and gain financial literacy. Yet when I discuss financial trauma with this audience, I'm met with often overwhelming realization—and sometimes resistance—that I have captured their experiences in a very succinct way. That I understand them on a soul level; and I do. I do because I don't discuss financial trauma through the lens of academia, financial therapy, or other formal institutions exclusively. I discuss financial trauma through the human experience, informed certainly by academic research and evidence-based practices, but punctuated by the realization that navigating economic systems can be traumatic in and of itself, and that experience can be further compounded not only by what we see, hear, are told, or otherwise experience directly but also by what our parents and their parents and their parents all experienced as well. In this book I'm going to introduce you to concepts around epigenetics and our genetic memories. I'm going to discuss various forms of trauma tied into a broad view of financial trauma that includes workplace trauma, vicarious trauma, racial trauma, and more. I'm going to introduce you to the Three Es, my framework for addressing and identifying financial trauma over several parts. I'm going to share stories of my experience and the experiences of clients, colleagues, and peers. I'm going to recommend and make suggestions that should be viewed as tools—not directives—that you can choose to incorporate into your life and practice as you feel comfortable and see fit.

Who This Book Is for (and Isn't)

I have a very specific audience in mind as I write this book. That said, if you don't fit that description, great! I hope you keep reading and get something from this work. If you are reading this book out of curiosity, to support me, as a mental health, financial services, or financial therapy peer, I thank you! You can proceed to read this book linearly (or feel free to skip around).

This book likely isn't for you if you refuse to acknowledge white supremacy as a pervasive and dominating ideology that has birthed such harmful systems as capitalism, racism, and the resulting imperialism, consumerism, and other systems of oppression and control we casually "opt in" to, either intentionally or by force. It's not for you if discussing topics like wealth distribution, systemic inequality, and racism is viewed as "morally irresponsible" and "dangerous" rhetoric. It's not for you if you feel that discussing socialist systems of economics is a threat to your individual efforts and "merit-based" upward social mobility. It's not for you if you feel that you can exist outside of community and that you are completely "self made," because no one is. We stand on the shoulders (or necks) of the people who have come before and sacrificed (or have been sacrificed) for us. If this book is not for you, then I especially encourage you to read it to wrestle through the discomfort, to acknowledge within yourself why you may be uncomfortable, and to perhaps open your mind to the tools and ideas I offer under "financial healing" and explore whether those tools make you feel better.

Ultimately, my goal with this book is to hold up a mirror. To make connections between concepts and to share stories and experiences and research to reach a broad audience of people with unmetabolized trauma related to finances. Whether you were introduced to this book in a classroom, a boardroom, social media, or word of mouth, this book is my life's work made manifest. This book seeks to empower you financially so that you may empower others.

Why Am I the Person to Talk About This

As I shared at the beginning of this preface, I've met financial trauma on several fronts. While many may acknowledge their financial hardships as personal failures and choose a route of extreme accountability to overcome them, many more do not. They feel stuck and swallowed by "the system," desperately grasping at straws to escape or eventually succumbing to its pull and resigning their efforts to hoping and praying they catch a "lick" that digs them out of their oblivion. In the face of my own financial struggles and triumphs, I have always made note of not only how I felt but how I perceived others to feel about it. The truth more often than not is that no one cares. No one cares about what ails you until you overcome it. But even in overcoming this, there are people who watch and who hold their breath to see that not only are you just like them but to justify their own self-doubt and battles for validation that victory (or failure) is a possible or likely outcome.

Working in and around financial services for more than a decade I got to observe how very similar we all are as humans with or without money. How much money amplified, how much money changed, how much money hid. I began to look at my individual success as a reflection of my community and then broader still as a reflection of the human condition. I started to draw parallels in experiences and to connect many of the dots I'll be connecting for you in this book. Admittedly, I've always had an interest in human behavior, but financial behavior captivated me. How did some people get rich, others get wealthy, and others stay stuck? Was I stuck to the same patterns and outcomes of my parents and their parents? Is "the man" holding me down? I started plotting a path to find out the truth long before any credentials, associations, awards, or publications came to me. In fact, I was something of an anti-credentialist for a time, believing that my experiences were enough. While discovering and finding professional homes in groups like The Financial Therapy Association, The Association for

Financial Counseling and Planning Education (AFCPE), and others have undoubtedly changed the trajectory of my professional
path, I was by and large doing this work before I joined any of
them. In short, I'm not going to talk to you like an academic or an
industry guy, but I do have the academic and industry support to
do so. You should listen to me on this topic because this topic is a
topic I've been living and breathing my whole life. While it's my
goal to pour everything I've got into this book, I know there will
be some things I leave out simply because I've forgotten more than
I'll ever know. This book has been generations in the making, and
I'm just honored and grateful that I get to be the conduit by which
its lessons are expressed.

Part I

EXPOSURE: INTRODUCING FINANCIAL TRAUMA

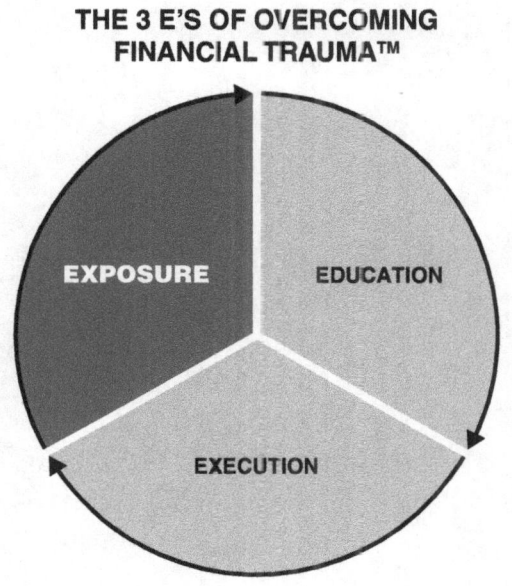

THE 3 E'S OF OVERCOMING FINANCIAL TRAUMA™

Chapter 1

Unpacking Generational and Genetic Financial Trauma

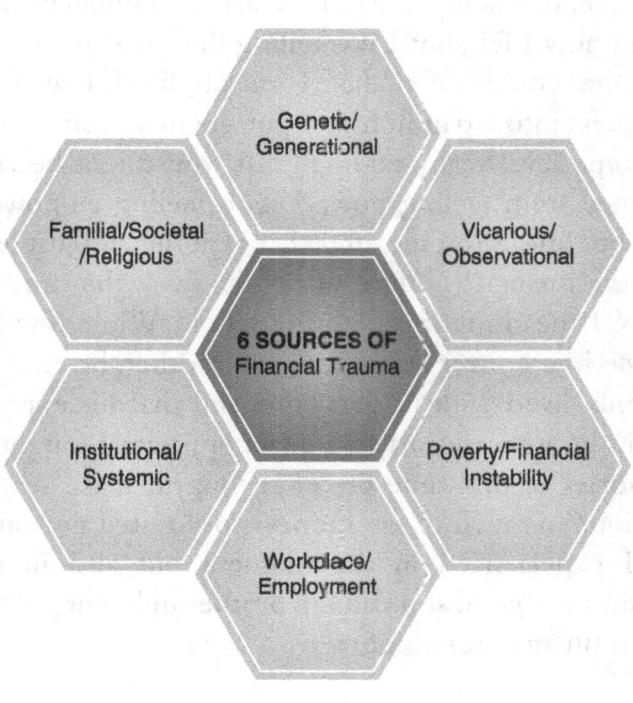

When I was in high school, I remember coming home one day to see an eviction notice taped to our front door. For context, the building I lived in had two sides, each with several floors—no elevator—and we lived on the first floor. You had to walk past our front door to get to the mailboxes and go to the next floor. I remember seeing that notice and experiencing a flood of emotions in less than 30 seconds. Fear, confusion, and embarrassment are among the most notable to me. "How many people saw this?" I thought to myself. I snatched the letter off the door so quickly because I didn't want anyone to know. I remember asking my mom if we were being put out, and her response was not to worry about it. I was the oldest of three at the time, and I don't ever remember sharing the news with my siblings. It felt not only like a personal secret but also a personal failure. It was the first time I remember feeling powerless financially. Not poor, just powerless.

In a 2019 TEDx talk I briefly described this experience to the audience. It was my first time sharing so publicly what happened and how I felt, but I was telling the story as a new homeowner. One could infer that I metabolized that feeling of powerlessness into a triumph that put me in a position of power, and on some level really zoomed out, you might be right. But that journey from feeling powerless to feeling empowered was anything but linear. You see, after that experience I just learned to navigate the financial systems of my family at the time—and by my family, I mean my mother's household. When revisiting this experience in a conversation with my brother, he reminded me that he only lived with us part-time and that his experience at my father's house was nearly the exact opposite. I fought through the memories of that time period, trying to make sense of this information. So much of my money story rested not only in the scarcity I experienced in the moment but also in rising to the occasion as a good son and big brother in helping steward the household finances for all of us.

In the process of that learning, despite never being told to, I began to make plans based on what I observed and experienced:

- Rent was too expensive to afford, so we needed Section 8.
- Groceries were too expensive to buy, so we needed food stamps.
- Food stamps were reloaded at the beginning of each new month, so I had to figure out how to help budget them so they would last.
- I'd buy store brand over name brand because it was cheaper.
- If the power goes out, then there's no hot water or lights. So we could use our gas stove to boil pots of water to bathe and use candles for light.
- If we didn't have enough money to wash clothes, we could wash our underwear in hot soapy water and hang it on the shower rod to dry before school the next day.

I had a solution to every problem as long as we had a place to stay. I felt like a savvy and responsible custodian of the household finances, and I was still just a teenager. I believed that when I was ready to live on my own, I would be prepared to do the same for my own finances. At this stage of acceptance and necessary navigation of my family's financial system, I began to shape my money story.

The thing about our money stories is that they are subjective and based on our individual observations and experiences. While much of what I've shared was true to me at the moment, it didn't occur to me until recently that these experiences were not objectively true of my family as a whole. As I shared, my immediate younger brother, for example, lived part-time with my father and was aware of the circumstances I helped to navigate, but not impacted in the same way because although he was part of this household, he was part of that one too. My younger sister, also present in the household, was too young to really understand the gravity of these experiences and thus never picked up the modeling around having Section 8 or food stamps. To her, we were just living life. Sharing this perspective on money stories is important because you can have multiple perspectives on money in the same household between spouses, between siblings, or parent to child.

Based on my experiences and the formation of my money story at the time, it didn't occur to me that it would be possible or likely that I could do anything but what I was witnessing and was a part of. That I could have a mortgage or even buy groceries without food stamps was such a far-off concept to me in my mid-to-late teens. I thought that by the time I lived on my own, I'd be so poor and struggling at first that if homeownership was possible, it would occur in my 40s and 50s and only if I went to a good school and maybe became a doctor or lawyer. The possibility seemed so distant, almost like it was a separate reality. In hindsight, I never thought it wasn't possible. I just thought, like winning the lottery, it wasn't very likely.

Throughout this book I'm going to provide you with various lenses to observe similar issues. You'll observe through psychological and neuroscience lenses. You'll observe through the lens of systems and socio-economics. You'll observe through somatic healing and financial therapy lenses. I want you to understand that my progression and your progression (or lack of progression) is not because we're smart, special, lucky, or hardworking *exclusively* but because of a combination of factors that have worked—or not worked—in our favor.

These perceived personal victories and failures have much deeper roots that we learn to expose or bury based on variables from a time even before we are born.

While you may or may not connect with or relate to the stories I tell, I want you to understand something extremely clear: an awareness of obstacles and stumbling blocks is not permission for you to give up; it's the opposite. As much as this book will seemingly poke and jab at the system, it demands your accountability.

What you do with the information in this book is on you, but my goal for you and anyone else who reads this book is to take you from feeling financially powerless due to past, present, or future financial trauma, to feeling financially empowered. This book is broken into three parts of my signature framework called **The Three E's Of Overcoming Financial Trauma™**, or simply "The 3E's™."

They stand for:

- Exposure
- Education
- Execution

If you're reading this book linearly, you will go through this framework up to the execution phase, where I will provide tools and perspective to take action—which I encourage you to do. Moving through this framework is what helped me go from "aspiring to be poor" to doing the work I do today. Ironically, as I'm writing this book I find myself combing through the framework in my own life and processing hidden or unresolved financial traumas that persist to this day. In that way we can say we are going on this journey together.

The first E in the framework is for **exposure**, which involves becoming aware a thing exists or afflicts you. In this part of the book, exposure is going to focus on providing you with terms, concepts, and definitions so that we can ensure we are on the same page, as well as providing a broad overview of some factors that contribute to financial trauma. It's important to point out the underlying systems that influence how people engage with money both broadly and directly: how people connect those external systems to the internal systems of our bodies and brain. Notice my use and focus on the word *system* as we will explore the concept of systems theory in becoming aware of and healing your relationship with money later.

The second E in the framework is for **education**, which involves some in-depth understandings of concepts and how things work. In addition to becoming aware a thing exists, you can understand how to navigate some of those things with tools, strategies, and resources at your disposal. Many people believe that increased financial literacy will solve issues of poor money management. While financial literacy has its place, you will see that financial literacy alone won't address the root of behavior or the impact of the systems you navigate. In the education section, we will examine financial literacy through a trauma-informed lens while also discussing successful navigation through systems.

The last E in the framework is for **execution**. This is arguably the most difficult phase of the framework and the context in which this book is being written. If nothing else, I want this book to empower you, the reader, to be mindful of obstacles that inflict financial trauma and to give you the tools to address financial trauma head on. During the execution phase of this book I will introduce you to methods for financial healing, exercises, and strategies you can execute on independently, in partnership with practitioners, and in community.

Author Note: I've created additional resources to accompany this book including videos, micro courses, and more. Scan the following QR code or visit RahkimSabree.com/resources to access them.

What Is Financial Trauma?

Financial trauma is any instance observed or experienced that has a negative impact on the way you view, interact with, or believe about money. When I came up with this definition, I was operating with the idea that I was the originator of the term.

As I began to socialize it and came up against clinical and academic definitions of financial (or money) trauma, I decided to double down on this definition as it encompasses so much more than the direct experiences one might have with money. This definition includes forms of vicarious trauma experienced by growing up in a poor environment—which may have a different effect than growing up poor—observing stressful, harmful, or abusive behaviors with money; being educated about how to use money through a lens of some financially traumatized person and thus inheriting or transferring their trauma onto you; and experiencing workplace or employment trauma, institutional trauma, religious trauma, or any other indirect (sometimes referred to as little "t" trauma) experience that influences your attitudes and beliefs about money.

Not only do these direct and indirect experiences shape our money stories but so do those of our parents, their parents, and their parents. Trauma—including financial trauma—can exist in our genetic memories and be passed down from generation to generation. The intergenerational transfer of trauma effects studied by Vivian Rakoff may have laid the foundation for what we now recognize as epigenetic studies credited to research by Rachel Yehuda. Yehuda and Lehrner cite Rakoff as the originator of the study of intergenerational trauma effects by quoting a paper that Rakoff wrote where he states that the children of Holocaust survivors displayed severe psychiatric symptomology (Yehuda & Lehrner, 2018). Yehuda's studies in epigenetics demonstrate that environmental factors, including stress, can affect the expression of genes not only in the individual experiencing the stress or trauma but also in their offspring.

Generational Money Beliefs

Have you ever felt like you needed to work harder than everyone around you? Do you feel pressured to take shortcuts by taking advantage of people? Do you think the acquisition of money is evil? Throughout my life I remember hearing some variation of all of these. In fact, I had a good friend who told me once that he views people as stepping-stones, and when asked if he viewed me as one, he told me straight up that he did. Did this make him a bad person? No, but it did provide insight into the lens through which he operated. A lens through which many of us secretly operate, for fear that should we be so honest in admitting it, we would be considered a bad person. The lens is one of scarcity, and it's that lens of scarcity that contributes to hoarding money (I need to get it), flaunting money (YOLO, I deserve this), and keeping up with the Joneses (I don't want people to think I'm poor). Extremes in behavior related to money can be due to dysregulation of emotions tied into generational coded messages about what money does or represents. When working with clients, one of the questions I like to ask is "What does money represent to you?"

For some of my clients, money represents security. ("I need money to feel secure.")

Money represents power. ("I need money so I can do/I need money so others can't do to me.")

Money represents status or respect. ("If I have money people will respect me.")

Tied into the concept of white supremacy, Black people may view having money as a leveling of the playing field. ("At least I'll be treated like a human being.") Is having money a prerequisite to being treated as human? We can look back at the historical mistreatment, colonization, exploitation, and abuse of Black bodies in the United States (including slavery) and draw direct ties to capitalism and a lack of security, respect, and power. Subconsciously, values related to working hard(er) can transfer across generations tied not only into survival via compensation but also the avoidance of abuse and the pursuit of freedom. Abstract? Perhaps in concept, but these are historical facts that without doubt have shaped the realities of generations of Black Americans who may in turn pass on these ideas as status quo unspoken rules for safety. In Chapter 4 we'll explore this a bit more. While many of the survival-based narratives we have around money are a reaction to larger systemic designs outside of our individual control, fortunately we can begin to reframe and heal some of the narratives around what money represents for ourselves through practices like affirmations that we'll explore in the chapters on financial healing in Part III of this book.

When I think about some of the most common financial habits inherited from previous generations that keep people stuck, I land on the concept of not talking about money. It's an odd thing really, when we think about how large a role money plays in our lives. Talking about the nuances of money (how to make it, how we use it, our mistakes with it, etc.) is often shrouded in shame, guilt, or frustration. It's one of the few things we learn about after we start using it. Sure, a lack of financial knowledge gets the brunt of the blame when it comes to bad financial habits, but let's be real; practical financial advice often sits behind someone's paywall. There is profit in financial illiteracy, and more than that, there is a sense of safety derived from one-upping someone who doesn't know the secrets to money, basically saying "If I know and they don't, there's more money for me. I'm better off. I'm more valuable."

This is a myth.

There's nothing wrong with admitting that the feeling you get when you know you make more money than someone is a good one. What about when you realize you make the most in your friend group, your immediate family, or your community? I'm not talking about your sense of obligation or the expectations they may have of you; I'm talking purely about knowing you make more.

It feels good, and there are those of us who will continue to chase that feeling without knowing why. That feeling is rooted in scarcity. This is the same scarcity that encourages you to hoard your money just in case, or to overspend because if you no longer have it, no one can ask you for it. You can talk about money, how you make it, use it, your mistakes with it, and you can establish and maintain financial boundaries.

Overspending might be another financial habit inherited from previous generations but not in the way you might think initially.

Certainly there are instances where overspending is a modeled behavior that gets passed on; however, with the FICO credit scoring model being introduced in 1989, the explosion of credit card debt is a relatively recent occurrence that blends the blatant cultural push for consumerism with the feelings of entitlement that says "I deserve this now." These feelings of entitlement may be a reaction to not having the means growing up to getting even the most basic of necessities when needed. Gradually, there was a cultural shift from using credit cards for emergencies to them being used for everyday purchases coupled with reward points and airline miles.

How Does Financial Trauma Manifest at a Genetic or Psychological Level?

Genetically, prolonged financial stress (such as poverty) can alter gene expression through epigenetics. If that stress is tied to perceptions of safety, security, and emotional regulation, especially through financial triggers, the expression of genes can be altered in future generations. The ripple effect of this can be devastating as heightened cortisol levels linked to obesity, eating disorders, and stress coping behaviors like gambling, alcohol addition, hypersexuality, and even the kinds of foods you eat for comfort or stress relief can compound not only physical disease but financial behavior as you have to spend money on all of these things to cope and/or remediate disease through expensive medications, procedures, or insurances.

When I was born, my mother was not much older than I was when I began to make the associations about money and survival I mention at the opening of this chapter. Her mother was about the same age as I was at that time when she gave birth to my mother. That's at least three generations of adult financial decision-making occurring in teenage bodies. That's three generations of stress hormones and financial struggle shaping the stories I told myself about money.

Psychologically you may demonstrate avoidant behaviors related to your finances such as not checking your bank account or credit score, not asking for fee refunds, and not opening mail.

This could contribute to feelings of shame or guilt as financial failures are often internalized as personal failures. It's important to highlight, however, that these feelings are not your fault. Cultural and systemic factors contribute to these cycles, especially in marginalized communities (we'll discuss this more in Chapter 5).

I think about the food we eat in the Black community called "soul food." I mean the baked macaroni and cheese, greens, candied yams, corn bread, and some kind of meat—usually pork or chicken. I think about the portion sizes we have piling our plates up high and the long-term impact of the high salt, high sugar, and high preservative content in the foods we eat when happy, when mourning or grieving, and when celebrating. I think about how cost-effective cooking these items in bulk are and how they are often paired with alcohol or sugary drinks like Kool-Aid, sweet teas, or lemonade. I think about how we trace diabetes, heart disease, high blood pressure, obesity, and certain cancers through our family lines as well. This ties directly into genetic expression with financial implications because it's not only what we bond over and trigger a dopamine response to, but it also makes us feel safe.

It makes us feel loved. It makes us feel like we're at home; even if we don't know anyone in the room with us, we instantly become cousins.

Realization

Financial trauma is not just a personal issue but an inherited one. We carry the financial wounds of our ancestors.

Declaration

"I will no longer accept the myth that financial trauma is just about bad decisions. It's systemic and generational."

Chapter 2

Vicarious Trauma and Financial Fear Through Observation

Client Story: Megan and Joel

Megan and Joel were a young couple living in New York City who came to me for financial therapy. They weren't on the same page financially and, despite being a high-income household, struggled with debt living paycheck to paycheck. When we initiated our session, Joel, the breadwinner, shared with me that he already knew what I was going to say about their situation: that they should know better, and that they did, both coming from a background in banking. Before letting him continue, I stopped him and assured him that he in fact did not know what I was going to say and that I was there to support him and his wife, not guilt or shame them into submission. As I watched his shoulders relax a bit, we started discussing the numbers and the subsequent issues behind them. When I asked him how he felt about all he had shared, he replied, "like an idiot."

Joel did most of the talking initially, sharing his goals, his values, and his financial behaviors with me. He valued being a provider and earning a majority of the household income. He valued spending time with friends and had poorly established financial boundaries when it came to social spending. I noticed when discussing going out to eat with friends specifically, there was a difference in opinion on splitting the bill evenly versus paying only for what they ordered. Megan felt it was rude not to split it evenly, and Joel's body language indicated he disagreed.

Megan was a creative entrepreneur, and a portion of Joel's income went to supporting her business. As they racked up credit card debt, balancing an expensive rent and lifestyle expenses, Joel's plate was full, and he didn't want to stay in this cycle of living paycheck to paycheck. I turned to his wife and asked her how she felt hearing all of this and if any of what he shared was new information.

She seemed a bit surprised that things were weighing on him the way they were but didn't seem to want to compromise on any of their spending habits and instead justified why they needed to maintain them. After a bit of hearing what she valued, her background in financial services, and the fluctuations in her entrepreneurial income, I got her to agree that their current lifestyle was not sustainable. I asked them about their plans for the future and whether they were planning for retirement.

This was where things began to unravel.

Joel shared that he knew it was important to plan for retirement, wanted to, but could not afford it due to the financial burdens he carried. Megan, on the other hand, did not believe in saving long-term due in part to her reaction to financial trauma she absorbed vicariously from her parents, which contributed to her chronic overspending and living in the moment approach to the household finances.

Megan didn't come from a struggling upbringing. Her family had moderate success in real estate. Delaying gratification, her parents built up a significant nest egg before deciding to indulge in the building of a family home. Unfortunately mid-build, her father had suffered a debilitating illness leaving him unable to work. With the family savings tied up in the unfinished home, the family was forced to liquidate assets at a loss. To make matters worse, she watched her mother spiral, turning to alcohol to cope with losing it all. Megan internalized the emotional scars of these experiences that would shape her approach to money in adulthood. Why save and delay gratification for the future when you could lose it all in an instant? Why not enjoy the money now?

This variable introduces a unique challenge in her marriage because Joel, concerned about his future, experiencing shame and guilt around the debt, and wanting to support his partner, was burning the candle at both ends.

Vicarious Financial Trauma

Vicarious financial trauma is the observation and internalization of someone else's financial pain, fear, or loss without direct experience.

The Adverse Childhood Experiences (ACEs) study revealed strong correlations between early trauma and long-term health and behavioral outcomes (Felitti et al., 1998). While financial trauma is not named explicitly in the original ACEs questionnaire, it does fit into categories like emotional neglect, household dysfunction, and parental mental health issues.

Witnessing financial struggle—especially as a child—can impact long-term money habits in a variety of ways. For some, it can create painful associations that encourage vigilance around money and/or disdain for people without it. Think about how you feel walking down a busy street and someone asks you for money. You see their clothes are a bit dated, and they may or may not have a smell of body odor—or worse. You might feel empathetic and want to help. You might feel offended and immediately disengage. You might make a split-second rationalization that their circumstances are a result of some personal failure and that they will use your money for drugs or alcohol. These feelings are reinforced by the criminalization of homelessness in public spaces. We tell ourselves things like "I don't want to end up like that," and we do all we can to avoid being associated with having no money. It can be assumed that the disdain we are socialized to have around those who struggle financially is really mislabeled fear of ending up the same.

Observation of financial struggle can also create associations between relationship dynamics such as who has more power and authority in a household or how expressions of love are interpreted.

Children especially may learn to make associations between money and love or affection when socialized with groups of children from different income brackets. The children with less may observe the children with more as being more valued or loved, especially if the things being measured include basic necessities such as food, clothing, or school supplies. I think about my own experiences in elementary school with Scholastic book fairs or school trips and what it felt like when I saw classmates going to the gift shops and buying souvenirs or school supplies. I wasn't the only one who had to sit out the shopping spree, and I remember finding common ground with other kids who couldn't afford to purchase anything. While I never doubted my parents loved me in the moments they had nothing to give, I do remember feeling extra loved when they gave me the few dollars they did have to get something.

Author Note: I've created additional resources to accompany this book including videos, micro courses, and more. Scan the following QR code or visit RahkimSabree.com/resources to access them.

Financial Socialization

As adults we observe how seemingly rich people treat others and are treated—they tend to always get their way, and people move with urgency, fearful of not meeting their needs. Meanwhile, if you are coming from a place of struggle, you are treated as a nuisance.

You are made to wait. You are talked down to and sometimes even yelled at.

These associations won't—often don't—correlate with the development of positive financial habits (especially if you don't know what positive financial habits even are) but rather teach people to hide their financial shortcomings by faking it until they make it while digging themselves deeper into debt regardless of increasing their income over time.

Financial fear through observation or vicarious financial trauma can be triggered directly by observing victims of institutional or interpersonal financial abuse. Redlining, discriminatory lending practices, denial of deposited funds, destruction of personal property, banks, and businesses (Tulsa Massacre, Freedman Bank, and similar), nonpayment of life insurance, repossession, eviction, etc., are just some historical and present-day examples of institutional abuse.

Interpersonal examples of financial abuse can include the observation of financial control within households. Using money to manipulate people to do things they otherwise wouldn't do or don't want to do by withholding access to resources and necessities or gift giving in exchange for certain outcomes can be examples of financial abuse. Taking advantage of elders via deception, coercion, or manipulation, forcing them to grant power of attorney or change the directions on wills or trusts also fall under this category. Opening service accounts like cable, electricity, phone, or credit cards in the name of an underaged child is also financial abuse.

The subsequent trauma (observed or experienced) is internalized and passed down via distrust, willful nonparticipation, hypervigilance in saving, money avoidance in overspending, or the acquisition of items with perceived value (like jewelry, cars, gold teeth) that can be pawned, sold, or worn/carried if there is a need to move in a hurry.

While clinical and traditionalist views of this behavior may point at deviations from normal and well-adjusted financial literacy practices, the behaviors are often survival based, cultural instructions coded in reaction to harm caused by the systems,institutions, and people many are told they should blindly trust and accept.

I don't want to get too far into this book before we examine financial trauma through a trauma responsive lens. That means we must dissect and analyze trauma research and the evolution of our understanding of trauma and how it expresses itself through human evolutionary fight-or-flight responses, through gene expression, and across generations. I'll go deeper on this topic in Chapter 7 when I discuss how financial trauma manifests in the mind and body, but for now we need to understand that when Joel said he felt like an idiot, he wasn't just being self-deprecating. That was shame talking, and shame is a trauma response. It hijacks logic, distorts memory, and overrides problem solving. The moment someone internalizes financial distress as a moral or intellectual failing, they lose access to the healing power of curiosity and self-compassion.

Financial trauma doesn't just live in the numbers; it lives in the nervous system. Joel's nervous system was sounding the alarm. He was caught in a cycle of hypervigilance racing to out-earn his stress—and his wife's nonchalance—without pausing to evaluate whether the emotional toll was compounding faster than his financial debt.

What he needed wasn't another budget app. He needed to feel safe, to be honest, to rest, and to make new financial decisions.

Megan, on the other hand, embodied avoidance. She'd built a belief system that centered a script that said enjoy it now before it's too late. Her "live for today" outlook wasn't rooted in irresponsibility—it was rooted in inherited fear. Her mother's breakdown, her father's illness, the unfinished home, were emotional blueprints etched into her money story.

Financial trauma is not always about what happened to you. Sometimes it's about what happened before you and how those echoes get embedded in behavior, preferences, and blind spots. These experiences left unchecked become part of the individual who then continues to pass on their trauma through their behaviors, their beliefs, and yes, their DNA.

Author Note: I've created additional resources to accompany this book including videos, micro courses, and more. Scan the following QR code or visit RahkimSabree.com/resources to access them.

The Fear You Didn't Choose (or Experience)

You don't have to live through a financial crisis to be scarred by one. Sometimes just watching someone else suffer is enough to plant the seed of fear. This is a quiet inheritance that you didn't ask for but absorbed anyway. It's not always a single moment but a series of silent observations that shape your money mindset in ways you don't even realize until your body starts reacting to it based on your financial socialization:

- The learned taboos around not discussing money
- Fear around negotiating salary
- Fear of credit cards and debt despite not ever having any

This is what vicarious trauma does. It teaches you to fear consequences you never experienced firsthand.

- Maybe your parents never said "We can't afford it," but you noticed tension when money matters were brought up.
- Maybe you witnessed the way people with money treated people who were struggling.
- Maybe a bill collector called your home and told you that if your parents didn't pay the bill they would be in trouble.

These observations teach your nervous system long before you get to a financial literacy course that not having money equals danger. Fear doesn't need full context. Just exposure.

There are people who insist on paying every bill early. Who never travel, even when they can afford it. Who stockpiled canned goods in the back of the pantry just in case. Sometimes it's emergency preparedness, sometimes it's trauma. The constant fear of a threat they're not prepared for.

This is dysregulation dressed up as responsibility.

I Grew Up in a Poor Neighborhood

I had a friend in high school whose parents owned a house. Out of the small crew of us, he was the only one who did. Every time we would go to visit, I noticed that he would get uncomfortable when we marveled at the artwork, decorations, and size of the interior of the home. He would get upset if we referred to him as "rich." He wasn't rich, his family was decently middle class, but he had more than me and my other friend did. I didn't realize it at the time, but he was ashamed of being viewed as having money. It made him stand out, it made him different, and he didn't want the extra attention.

When conversations on money are had, it's usually in the context of rich versus poor. There aren't often stories of the individuals who grow up adjacent to the rich families or adjacent to the poor ones. You don't hear about the impact of being well-off in a poor neighborhood or environment. These positions have profound effects on how you relate to money, understand money, and use money socially.

- You can have money and experience vicarious financial trauma by proximity.
- You can have money and experience financial trauma despite your income.

Financial trauma doesn't discriminate.

We don't just learn about money from our own experiences—we absorb it from what we witness, what we survive, and what we're never allowed to talk about. Megan and Joel weren't broken; they were rehearsing a trauma script they didn't know they'd inherited. In a world where financial struggle is moralized and personal failure is highlighted as a moral one, vicarious trauma is present, pervasive, and imminent.

The goal here isn't to judge or fix—it's to see. Once you can name the fear, the patterns begin to lose their power.

My "rich" friend used his access to money to fit in. He wore the name brand clothes, had the new game consoles and the cool sneakers. Although he knew he stood out, he found ways to establish safety by giving to others. Whether that looked like providing them with an experience they didn't have via access to the games he had, or "buying" friendships, I don't remember there being a time he was ever targeted for having what others did not. I imagine his parents worked hard to provide him with the life he enjoyed and through no fault of their own didn't realize how he struggled to reconcile his privilege with others that didn't have the same. I wonder today what his money story looks like. How access and exposure in the way he experienced it influenced his behavior with money as an adult. If our time together was any indication, he may have learned through the establishment of his own safety that money can be used to make people "like you."

Financial Abuse and Power

People learn through observation first and doing second. Absent the contextual nuances of morality and social order, it's not unreasonable to infer that people will do what is easy and what works. Unfortunately, the subjugation of others for money and with money has proven effective across generations going back thousands of years. Knowing that money or the idea of money is linked to livelihood, influence, and control makes it easy for those with money to abuse and exploit those with less or without.

Financial trauma stemming from financial abuse affects not only the target of abuse but everyone that target touches, including the individual carrying out the abuse. The harmful reinforcement of money ideals that make it a weapon to begin with codifies the abusive behavior in the abuser, directly harms the individual abused, and if observed by a third party (like a child or dependent) can influence the ways in which they perceive or interact with money. Unfortunately, the only things shielded from the vicarious trauma fallout are the institutions built on the foundations of financial trauma.

The good news is that institutions are run by people, and people can be healed from trauma. In Chapter 10 I'm going to discuss what this healing can look like for banks and financial services providers looking to reengage with communities impacted by decades of mistrust.

And while not an excuse of the behavior, it's important to note that those who inflict financial trauma (or trauma in general) are likely reacting to trauma they've inherited or have had inflicted onto them, creating a vicious cycle that may have a hazy point of origin.

Chapter 3

The Trauma of Poverty and Financial Instability

Y ou may be asking yourself who doesn't have financial trauma? That is not only an excellent question but an appropriate first step toward examining the effectiveness of the systems we navigate economically, politically, socially, and internally. In this part of the book, the purpose is to trigger or introduce you to a pattern of thought you may not have previously acknowledged or considered when examining your relationship with money. If you were taught about money growing up or even in your formal income earning years, why were you not taught to conceptualize it through the lens of your personal psychology, cultural values, or financial systems? If you were not taught about money growing up and instead adopted social taboos around the appropriateness of discussing your finances as something you avoid—along with religion and politics—was that accidental or is it by design?

Ecological systems theory explores how an individual develops within a series of systems that both shape the individual and respond to influences from their presence. That's to say that to understand an individual's development, beliefs, and values, it is important to consider the context of their interactions (Durband et al., 2019).

I've seen many adults share how much richer their life is when they leave their hometowns. I've also observed the feelings of isolation one feels when they disconnect from their support systems by way of physical proximity. In the fall of 2010, I left behind my brothers and sister, dad, grandfather, grandmother, my friends, and a neighborhood I grew up in to move across the country with my mother, who had a vision for a new life. For eight months I existed in isolation from the things and people I knew, to try to start over. While I had left behind many painful memories related to money, I also left behind many positive ones related to safety and security—or at least the perception of those things—via familiarity. As a young man I couldn't fully appreciate the opportunity in front of me because despite making the choice to leave with my mother, I was still totally dependent on her and opting into a new family system that I still had no control over. How many times have you been faced with an opportunity by choice, circumstance, or both where you resisted because it was unfamiliar to you? Why does it often take multiple attempts for victims of domestic abuse to leave their abuser? How do people choose to exploit the benefits of Section 8, food stamps, and welfare generation after generation? I can tell you that in many of these instances, it's not for not wanting to. It's not even for not trying to escape it. In 2023 I presented for the National Association of Social Workers (NASW) where I discussed with the clinicians some of the systemic issues social workers face with their clients specifically around money. The topic of fear came up when it came to certain clients increasing their income due to what is known as a benefits cliff. The benefits cliff refers to the loss of public assistance benefits due to a small increase in income. The loss in benefits is often significantly greater than the gain in income, resulting in financial distress.

Intuitively, one would think that any opportunity to increase income would be embraced with open arms. What many of the social workers identified with, however, was that their clients sometimes depended on certain government programs that helped them pay rent or put food in the house and that by accepting a higher-paying job, they would no longer be eligible for those programs. In doing the math, sometimes the increase in pay wouldn't justify what they lost in benefits, and therefore mathematically didn't make sense. The fear these clients experience is not an unreasonable one. Furthermore, they may be navigating guilt and shame related to that fear because they may want to do better but simply can't afford to. The trauma of poverty and financial instability creates a ripple effect that is anything but rational. Even after escaping the reality of poverty, the post-traumatic stress of it can persist, driving financial decision-making and habits that shape social interactions, political beliefs, and ideas about safety and power tied to money.

During my period of eight-month isolation, I gained weight from indulging in food as pleasure and a companion. I moved from a walkable city in Mount Vernon, New York, to San Antonio, Texas, where you needed a car to get around. I was making less money working a seasonal retail job than I had been making as a part-time permanent employee at a grocery store, and I had no car.

I felt stuck.

I became very active on social media and used Skype for video calls—this is before we had FaceTime and video conferencing platforms like Zoom—to stay connected to my friends, but I was lonely and alone. Just when I finally started to get acclimated to the new normal by making new friends and looking at colleges to transfer my credits to, my mother came to me with more news: "We're moving again." This time, it was closer to home but still a bit of a hike. The day after my 21st birthday, I flew back to New York for the summer while she and her partner prepared to make the move. In hindsight, I am reminded of the following passage from *The Body Keeps the Score* that references parallels between the author's observation of his patients and a study done with mice related to stress:

> "Scared animals return home, regardless of whether home is safe or frightening. I thought about my patients with abusive families who kept going back to be hurt again. Are traumatized people condemned to seek refuge in what is familiar? If so, why and is it possible to help them become attached to places and activities that are safe and pleasurable?" (Van Der Kolk, 2015)

From a psychological perspective, it could be assumed that I wanted to return to what was familiar to me. From a systems lens, I was opting into a familiar system. One variable of note in my return home that summer was that during the eight months prior, I had for the first time ever lived in a house with my own room and a yard in a residential community, and the apartment I would stay in was in a housing project with pissy stairwells and elevators that got stuck . . . but hey, I was home.

Author Note: I've created additional resources to accompany this book including videos, micro courses, and more. Scan the following QR code or visit RahkimSabree.com/resources to access them.

Poverty is as much a state of being as it is a system. I say it's a system because it is by design. No one accidentally falls into poverty, and no one chooses it. In the past I would break down the words poverty and wealth to their origin with poverty referencing a "wretched state." While we can choose to change our mindset, sometimes we can't immediately change the conditions that breed and foster that mindset. In Chapter 5 I will focus more directly on institutional and systemic contributors to financial trauma, but for now the point I want to illustrate is that systems theory explains there are multiple things at play sometimes simultaneously, others in a sequence that influences the state of poverty as a function of the mind (internally) and as a function of circumstances (externally). What's worse is that often we are navigating systems and following familiar patterns that may hurt us unknowingly. These systems can become blurred and make up what we call *culture* or *cultural norms*. Poverty environments often create financial trauma even if you're only poverty adjacent. In other words, someone might grow up in an environment that could be described as impoverished or "the hood" and start to pick up the nuances of behavior, thoughts, and beliefs that are central to the culture of that environment. Influenced by the spirit of survival mode, they may not necessarily have painful money memories or experiences directly but can take on attitudes rooted in scarcity that bend their reality such that they think in much the same ways as their neighbors who experience poverty do.

Sometimes this can create trauma bonds that look like friendship because we recognize and relate to each other's struggle. We may anchor in that bond and later feel remorse when we realize that the root of our friendship was a shared trauma and nothing else—or worse when the root of our friendship was that shared trauma but we've moved past it and they have not. This is why I say it's a *state of being*. It's not just some negative number in your bank account or the absence of assets. Poverty is so pervasive that even when you escape physical scarcity, command a high income, and start to accumulate assets, you can still have a poverty mindset—and it's not your fault.

Let me repeat that: it's not your fault.

I want to share an experience I had at one of my workshops with the members of the audience. I was holding a workshop on money stories and discovering the root of financial behavior where I explored not only the audience's upbringing and environmental factors that influence what they believe about money but also their present-day influences. I explained that corporations have invested in understanding our behavior when it comes to spending so much so that they can with near certainty predict how we will spend money with them next. In the book *The Power of Habit*, the author Charles Duhigg describes how companies like Target can even predict when a woman is pregnant based on the data tracking and analysis (Duhigg, 2014). I highlighted how companies like Robinhood invest in gamification to trigger a dopamine dependency that nudges consumers in a particular direction using their phone's notifications. One participant shouted out, "I got a notification from McDonald's while I was at the gym!" We laughed over the complimentary small fries offer before I let them know these things are not by accident. The scary part? Most consumers have no idea they've opted into this system and are therefore doomed to being funneled down its corridors.

The Illusion of Choice

Edward Bernays, known as the father of public relations (and unironically the nephew of Sigmund Freud) helped to revolutionize how companies' market to consumers. His work informed how advertisers learned to connect feelings with their products. One of his most well-known campaigns involved connecting feminine attractiveness to smoking cigarettes. If companies can predict what you'll spend your money on before you spend it and can influence the feelings of desirability, love, acceptance, etc., by connecting their products to your emotional outcomes, how much of your financial decision-making is truly your choice?

If governments and politicians can exploit public desires, fears, security, and education by leveraging or building on Bernays's strategy, what can be assumed about the illusion of choice present in voting decisions, what and where to buy, and how to treat other people who resist or exist outside of the status quo? Although these questions are being asked as a rhetorical hypothetical, the unfortunate truth is that this is our reality and has been for quite some time.

While the McDonald's app mentioned in my workshop may or may not have known the participant was at the gym when it triggered a notification offering him free fries, the notification itself was no accident. It was nudge, and we are overwhelmed with nudges every day.

Sticking to a budget isn't hard because you're bad with money. Sticking to a budget is hard because you're constantly being targeted to spend the money you do have on things to fill needs, needs you didn't realize you had because they are needs you are told to have through advertising. These "needs" are really your reaction to being dysregulated and overstimulated. Your body responds to stressors by engaging in fight, flight, freeze, or fawn responses, and thanks to advertising psychology the solution to those stress responses often rests in you spending more money, sometimes money you don't even have.

What does this have to do with poverty and financial instability though?

What I'm illustrating here is that poverty is not only a state of being influenced by your mindset, but that it's a state of being curated externally as you are hijacked physiologically, psychologically, and financially. While the choices you make are yours alone, very often you and others like you don't realize they're making a choice at all.

In summary, poverty and financial instability keep you in a state of fear or panic so that you might "return home" regardless of whether it's safe or frightening. You experience guilt or shame for reverting to familiar patterns without understanding why and many times feel stuck in your attempts to make an escape due to the illusion of choice. The worst part? Even when/if you get the high-income job, win the lottery, gain an inheritance, or otherwise escape fiscal poverty, your poverty mindset follows you at a higher tax bracket.

Chapter 4

Human Capital, Human Cost: Workplace and Employment Trauma

As an employee, I've always been results driven, looking for the quickest pathways to career progression. I took pride in the titles, responsibilities, and pay that would result from my efforts. I was a team player, strategic, a great collaborator, and a leader of people and processes. I was often the youngest leader on a team and one of the most respected. I didn't just drink the corporate Kool-Aid—I chugged it. Often encouraging others who looked like me to learn how to "play the game," I made associations between my rapid career progression and my value, always chasing the next promotion and pay increase.

My interactions with supervisors, managers, and executives resulted in similar responses; they all seemed to see some version of themselves in me. I was rewarded with accolades, recognition, and access to many of them in ways my colleagues were not. Superficial mentorships, superficial responsibilities, and stretch assignments weren't uncommon, but I ate it all up. With each promotion and raise I moved one more step away from the scarcity of my childhood—or so I thought. With each change in title I could go out into the marketplace and command greater respect. In hindsight, I spent more time in my career as a supervisor or manager than I did as an individual contributor.

What I didn't realize at the time was that in addition to my ambition there was a deeper longing to establish safety and security. Although my family circumstances had changed by this point and I was earning money of my own, the echos of past financial trauma didn't just evaporate into thin air. It lurked behind my ambitions, bringing me further away from the instability of my teenage years but haunting me in a way that made me keenly aware that I never wanted to be poor again. It was easy to conclude through this lens that survival comes from performance because performance is frequently tied into pay.

If you're an HR professional reading this, I might sound like someone you've worked with. Someone you provided feedback on around compensation and merit increases. I might sound like someone you've interviewed and/or hired. It will be important for you to seek out and acknowledge the drivers for employee performance as part of a broader trauma response that is not singularly tied into a good mesh of company culture and candidate. Company culture may exacerbate this trauma, which can lead to early burnout, turnover, and decreased employee morale. In Part III of this book I'll focus on financial healing, which will include how to build a financial wellness program at your organization. Very often you, or someone on your team, is the gatekeeper for instigating necessary change.

If you're a first-generation high-income earner reading this, I might sound like you. Examine where there might be similarities in our stories. Maybe the drivers for performance in your career don't come from a place of financial struggle but from a place of financial fixation. Examine what it means to get the raise, the promotion, the corner office, or to make partner, become VP, or get hired as CEO, to you. Hold on to these thoughts as you work through this chapter and revisit them throughout this book.

In either case, I want you to know something that took me a long time to reconcile within myself: everything I was taught through observation, positive reinforcement, the superficial titles and responsibilities, the smiles and handshakes, all of it, was wrong—at least through the lens of financial trauma. The corporate structure uses scarcity and competition in a way that exploits your trauma, compounds it, or introduces it to you for the very first time. Some may call it a necessary evil or may choose to focus rather on the positives. You may truly enjoy what it is you do—and there is no shame in that—but what I've come to realize about financial trauma is that it is a really great fuel source for corporations and their career progression models because the closer you get to the top, the more of yourself you have to give to climb higher. You become viewed as human *capital* rather than a human being. The illusion of security you accept in the form of a paycheck, stock options, and paid time off is just reinforced until something or someone breaks it. Financial trauma can make that feel necessary, when the reality is it is not.

> "You become viewed as human *capital* rather than a human being."

It makes sense though, doesn't it? The United States has a capitalism-driven economy that thrives on scarcity and consumerism. It *needs* people like me and you to believe in the salvation of a bigger paycheck, because outside of covering basic survival needs, there's always something else to spend money on. I'll discuss capitalism in more detail in the next chapter, but for now I want to shine a light on workplace and employment trauma and the toxic relationship between corporate America and its workers.

There's an uncomfortable but necessary truth here: the workplace borrows from the rationale of chattel slavery. In both systems, human value is measured in productivity. Resistance is punished. Identity is suppressed. And rest? Rest is rebellion. The term *human capital* doesn't just reduce people to economic units—it echoes a legacy where Black bodies were literally capital. Today, your labor might be compensated, but your full humanity still isn't always welcomed.

Author Note: I've created additional resources to accompany this book including videos, micro courses, and more. Scan the following QR code or visit RahkimSabree.com/resources to access them.

The Breaking Point

In February 2021 I shared this tweet out of frustration on the job:

> "Corporate America's toxic trait is guilting you for wanting more for yourself while simultaneously gaslighting you into thinking your skills, talents, and experiences are worth less than you deserve. 😣"

I don't remember what exactly caused the frustration in that moment, just that it was the culmination of things that resulted in my quitting three months later with no notice and no backup plan. In the months and years following my departure, I've had time to untangle the mess of feelings and emotions that influenced that decision. While some would paint it as a "rage quit," it was anything but. It was a calculated and necessary move at protecting not only my mental well-being but my physical and spiritual well-being as well.

I remember vividly two instances where my fight-or-flight response was activated due to direct attacks to my livelihood at work. The latest (resulting in my departure from corporate America) became so antagonistic that I began to develop physical rashes on my body from the stress. I was asked repeatedly to justify my role and responsibilities in an environment where layoffs were being announced and rumors of a merger loomed. I was given tasks outside of the scope of my work, publicly humiliated via email broadcasts, and bullied with questions about my outside business interests. Veiled threats to my employment were made wrapped in corporate phrasing that could be hidden behind as innocent or draped in assumed positive intent. I was told that "if I had a manager who asked me to do something I'd try to find ways to make them happy" or penalized for just doing my job but not anticipating ways to take on additional responsibility and go above and beyond.

I knew the game; you probably do too.

"Per my last email."

"Let's take this offline."

"All hands on deck."

"We'll circle back."

While this phrasing alone is not weaponized, if you've been on the receiving end of vocabulary like that (or the one dishing it out), then you know the connotations they carry. The week I decided I was going to quit I remember the strong feeling of fear in the pit of my stomach. I told myself things like how irresponsible it would be and how disappointed people would be, including my parents. I thought about how I've always done the right thing, the right way from being on the honor roll to joining clubs, from volunteering to sports teams, to mentoring others. I had convinced myself entirely that coloring outside the lines was not me and that by making this decision I'd be letting everyone, including myself, down.

Then I thought about the metallic taste in my mouth every morning during conference calls. The forced "good mornings" when I was having anything but. The frustration I would feel when certain names came across my caller ID or instant messages and the subsequent forced pleasant voice I would put on.

I no longer recognized myself.

Before I quit my job I discussed pursuing a discrimination suit with a colleague who worked at the same company. I laid out my plan and all the ways in which I was being targeted and how I didn't feel comfortable going up the chain of command because I was lower on the totem pole and no one would believe me.

What the colleague said to me changed the trajectory of my life. They told me that I wasn't the first person to feel this way or attempt that strategy. The company had lawyers for this and I would lose. When I asked what they advised, they said:

> "Say yes sir, no sir. Yes ma'am, no ma'am until you get a promotion or find something else."

That statement caused a visceral reaction inside of me to which I replied, "Nah, that ain't in my blood." They acknowledged they heard me, and I said again, "Nah, that ain't in my blood!"

Immediately after making that declaration I felt the activation of raw energy in the center of my chest so strongly I remember feeling like I was going to cry. It was as if my ancestors in that moment all cheered me on and affirmed my decision not to equate my value with my title, position, or pay but rather to do what was best for me in that moment.

On May 28, 2021, I quit my job around 9:30 a.m. effective immediately with no notice and no backup.

I fired my boss.

I'm not encouraging you to quit your job, especially not the way I did, but I am sharing that by quitting my job and pursuing entrepreneurship, I had inadvertently begun a healing process that exposed some of the money narratives I held that influenced not only my personal finances but how I perceived myself in comparison to other people and how I approached career progression.

To a degree, every workplace is going to have a measure of toxicity to it because you are trading your most valuable commodity for something infinitely less valuable in order to survive. We all have to work in some capacity to make money. It's what you've been socialized to do your entire life from the moment you enter grade school. You learn to compete, to take tests, to follow instructions, to play well with others, to submit to authority. You learn about authoritative hierarchy: the teacher is your direct manager; the principal is the CEO. The teacher's pet becomes the line leader, and we see this repeated with our team leads and those up for promotion. We learn to fawn as a mechanism of survival.

Navigating the Second Self

Fawning as a trauma response is clinically recognized as a people-pleasing function stemming from childhood abuse or trauma. It's a disassociation of sorts from your own emotional and psychological needs to establish a sense of safety. I first encountered the phrase *financial fawning* while participating in *The Trauma of Money*, a psychoeducational program (and book) that certifies professionals and organizations in trauma-sensitive approaches to money. While financial fawning refers to using money as a tool to seek security and attachment, how you go about acquiring money in the first place also requires a great deal of fawning behaviors, especially for Black and other minority bodies.

Famously referred to as *code-switching*, Black employees may employ a fawning strategy that involves talking in a pitch or tone that is perceived as less threatening, often higher and slower than their regular speaking tone. In some of my friend groups, we'll jokingly (not so jokingly) laugh as we refer to it as our "white voice." Black people don't have the monopoly on this fawning behavior in the workplace, and tone of voice is not the only example. Black, Latina, and multi-ethnic women, for example, have adopted ideals around professionalism when it comes to things like how they wear their hair. They may straighten their hair, lighten the color, or avoid protective styles like braids or locs because it has historically been considered less professional. Abandoning pieces of yourself for the sake of professionalism might feel like a matter of choice and being a team player. It might feel like you can manage the two different versions of yourself. You might be really good at it; I know I was. The problem doesn't lie in your strength or mental endurance though; it lies in a system that forces you to engage in economic survival strategies where you have to be other than your authentic self in order to get paid. When your income, and by extension your security, is tied to being nonthreatening and palatable, financial trauma shows up in the illusion of choice you might feel you are making.

When I first started my banking career, I was 21 years old. I had tattoos and wore earrings at the time. My tattoos were never visible because I wore long-sleeve button-up shirts, and my earrings were studs, appropriate per the dress code I poured over when I got hired. One day while standing in the bank lobby, my manager came to me and told me that wearing earrings was unprofessional. I removed them and stopped wearing them to work, thinking I would just put them back in when I left the office and take them off when I returned. The thing is, between the ages of 21 and 31, I can probably count on my hands how many times I wore earrings after that. If you're wondering why this is relevant, I want to point out that this is not at all about me wearing earrings. Hearing that something about the way I presented in my daily life, something that at that time was a part of my identity, was considered unprofessional had a profound impact on me throughout the rest of my career that echoed into my personal life. I didn't stop wearing earrings because I grew out of the look. I stopped wearing earrings because I spent a majority of my time during the week at work, and it became more convenient to just leave them off altogether than toggle between these two identities.

Later in my career I would work in a relaxed call center environment where employees could wear jeans and dress business casual. For the entire first year of my employment, I would wear a suit jacket over my shirt, and I would not wear short sleeves no matter the weather. I was praised for my professionalism. I believed that by wearing a jacket, it signaled to others my authority as a leader and served to enhance my professional brand. The first time I took off my jacket and wore short sleeves there was a rumble in my department. I had tattoos! I wasn't wearing a jacket! I turned this into a teachable moment for the staff there and explained my reasoning as protecting my brand. I explained that I was conscious of the fact that I was not only the youngest manager in the department but also one of few Black ones. That had I showed up with my tattoos visible any sooner than I did, I believed that no one would necessarily say anything about it to me out loud, but that there would be thoughts about it for sure. Those thoughts could impact how I was perceived as credible, as competent, as professional. I explained that by waiting, most of the leaders and decision-makers I'd interacted with had a chance to see just how credible, competent, and professional I was without making biased judgments based on my appearance alone. Unfortunately, despite this fact, there would still be judgments made and held no matter what I did because there are some things about myself like my name, the color of my skin, my age, etc., that I simply cannot conceal. It was a great social experiment but a necessary one because as I shared these things and sparked discussion among our team members, there was also an acknowledgment that much of what I was saying, while uncomfortable, was true.

Conditioned Compliance

In the workplace, religious practices like prayer or fasting, for example, may be hidden or altogether avoided. Age, relationship status, even disability may be masked in an effort to avoid standing out and being noticed as different despite the legal protections around discrimination and bias. The idea that you have to work twice as hard to get just as far in addition to balancing a nonthreatening identity creates what has been famously referred to by W.E.B. Du Bois as a second self or double consciousness. Despite commitments to initiatives around diversity, equity, and inclusion by some organizations, many marginalized people don't just view their acceptance as a corporate "check off the box" initiative. Safety for them is not tied into the statistics and stakeholder value associated with having a diverse team. Seeking safety remains the top priority in these spaces that at best force you to be hyperconscious of your noticeable differences and at worst force you to drink the Kool-Aid in such a way you forget your differences altogether. You might be puzzled by that last statement. Why would it be worse to forget your differences? The truth is that while you may forget your differences, very often your peers will not. It will be those differences that inform the lens by which your performance, competency, professionalism, and engagement are viewed when necessary to remind you of your place. This is a place of compliance that we are taught to cycle through for most of our lives. Deviations from it are penalized with varying degrees of ridicule and public shaming. It is no coincidence that the same compliance you are socialized to adopt throughout your school years becomes the compliance by which you are expected to engage at your places of employment, or the compliance you are expected to demonstrate in the presence of law enforcement, medical staff, politicians, etc. While undoubtedly part of corporate norms, this compliance (and the power you surrender around your bodily autonomy and identity) is part of a larger systemic mechanism that is built on institutional trauma, which I'll be discussing in the next chapter.

Realization

Workplaces contribute to financial trauma through pay inequity, toxic work cultures, and financial stressors.

Declaration

I will no longer accept workplaces that ignore financial trauma while demanding peak performance.

Chapter 5

Institutional and Systemic Financial Trauma

My grandfather always made it a point to ensure we had two educations—the one we got in school he referred to as "his-story" and the one we got at home, true history. I was never puzzled as to why the two educations were necessary; I was however intrigued by the fact so many of my peers never got both. I didn't grow up believing that my salvation or safety existed in whiteness. I never believed in a fat white man in a red suit coming to deliver presents on Christmas. I never believed Columbus discovered America or that the pilgrims were friends to the natives. I never believed in a white woman swapping out my lost teeth for money. I never envisioned any version of God with blond hair, blue eyes, or white skin. My parents (rightfully) took the credit for any gifts they purchased for my siblings and me, and the collective effort between my father and grandfather ensured that my self-esteem and confidence came from within and not via my proximity to whiteness or status quo expectations. Eurocentric "white" standards were not my standards. I was taught to believe in Black excellence before it became a social media hashtag.

And, I was encouraged to share it. "Each one teach one, each one reach one. If you know, teach. If you don't know, learn." It was a mantra I grew up reciting.

As young as the third and fourth grades my grandfather would pick me up from school and ask me, "Did you sneeze in anyone's face today?" Sneezing was a metaphor for spreading knowledge by using "good germs" so that they would spread. Sometimes sneezing would look like a casual conversation with a peer. Other times it would look like challenging a teacher on a piece of information shared with the class. Where most students are taught blind compliance, I was taught to question everything. Be respectful, but question everything. I was taught the meaning of words by their definition. I was taught to read for comprehension and asked for my interpretation on the things I read. When I would ask a question about how or why something was, my grandfather would frequently reply, "What does your brain tell you?" I center my father and grandfather in these stories so frequently because there are a lot of little Black boys and girls who grew up without them. We often see examples in popular culture of the maiden, mother, and crone archetype, seeing the feminine in various states of development. Less common do we see examples of the three stages of masculinity in harmony with one another. In making note of this observation one has to ask, are Black men just unwilling to be part of their children's lives or is it the system?

Author Note: I've created additional resources to accompany this book including videos, micro courses, and more. Scan the following QR code or visit RahkimSabree.com/resources to access them.

I've heard whispers and declarations of a system designed for me to fail all my life. This system disproportionately targets, jails, and oppresses Black men—and by extension anyone without a proximity to whiteness. I've never been arrested and have had very few negative interactions with the police, yet when I see the flashing lights of a police car in my rearview mirror or even recognize that a police car is behind me I feel a subconscious freeze in my body. I've had customers and coworkers remark on how incredibly articulate I am, question where I went to school, or remark on my kindness and manners as if I'm not expected to speak great English, have an education, or be polite. If propaganda is America's biggest export, then racism is the vessel it's transported through. This racism is embedded in the institutions and fabric of American culture from the constitution to the legal system, from educational institutions to medicine, from advertising to the way we spend our dollars.

The system, being so painfully present, always seemed invisible to white people, though. It's spoken of as if it's some sort of boogeyman and that the cheat code to comfortably living within this system rests in both ignoring it and radical compliance (even if you are being oppressed). Many marginalized people subscribe to the model minority myth that pits minority groups against one another in an effort to attain white acceptance. Within the white supremacy system, Black people are a permanent underclass making other minority groups (including diasporic Africans) distrusting of Black Americans. The only feigned exception to this rule rests in money. Specifically, if a Black American becomes wealthy, they are considered the exception and not the rule. They are viewed as not being like the others. They are tolerated—not accepted—in white and other minority spaces. They are tokenized and used to prop up diversity quotas and examples of success.

Financial institutions like banks, lenders, and credit bureaus are often framed as neutral gatekeepers of access and opportunity. But for many they've been instruments of exclusion and exploitation. From historic and present day redlining to predatory lending, these

systems have codified bias into status quo. While efforts have seemingly been made to rectify wrong doings, those efforts have been
made from a position of economic strength garnered from the
exploitation in such a way that it couldn't hardly be repaid.

Racism from this perspective can't be viewed as an oversimpli-
fied bigotry or prejudice against Black people (or anyone who isn't
white). Racism has to be viewed through the lens of the systems it
permeates to maintain status quo whiteness at the top in relation
to everything and everyone else.

There was a time in my life where money made me feel powerful.

I could go into any store with my Amex card and command
respect. Money gave me permission to talk back, to ask to speak to
a manager, to file a complaint if I felt I didn't like the service I
received or the way I was treated. Money made me feel like though
the system existed, I was winning at it. The statistics didn't matter
because I made my own choices. I was the master of my circumstances. Despite having the two educations growing up, I started to fall
into a trap that many successful first-generation high earners fall into:
I viewed the system as a singularly race-based boogeyman that in
the liberal north hadn't touched me often at all. It lurked beneath
the shadows of micro aggressions but rarely if ever was it outright
blatant in its expression. I didn't immediately recognize its design
as the multiheaded monster it was, one that was race and class
based and one that dually despised you if you were not white and
if you were poor.

My experience is shared by many high-income earners. We
subscribe to the belief that our financial privilege somehow acts as
armor to the other "isms." I remember watching an interview
where rapper Lil Wayne stated something to the effect that he
didn't believe racism existed anymore because when he performs
for white audiences, they love him. That money or class ascension
makes you immune to the race-based discrimination is a semicon-
scious myth in minority communities, and that is because race is
tied into classism and capitalism as tentacles of the white supremacy power structure we refer to as "the system."

We are often taught through advertising and real-world economics about supply and demand. The more scarce something is, generally the more expensive that thing becomes. Whether it's an item of status or survival, an experience, or access to resources and education, there is always a premium tier. This manufactured scarcity is weaponized in a way that induces your trauma responses to constantly feel like you are missing out on something you need and that by spending the money you acquire in exchange for your time, you can be better, smarter, more attractive, find love, establish security, be healthier, be happier, or at the very least pretend to be those things. It's a vicious cycle because once you spend the money, you move on to the next thing seeking validation in the advertisements and approval of your peers and those who surround you. You bond with people like you with similar struggles and triumphs. You compare what you have to what they have, not wanting to be the one left behind and engage in silent competition. The industries you consume from collect your years of life in the form of currency to increase their profits while you champion capitalism. It's the worst kind of vampirism yet you want to be turned because you would rather be the hunter than the hunted.

As a financial educator I've seen my fair share of marketing that promotes not only wealth building but generational wealth building. It speaks to that one risk taker. The one in the family that's misunderstood. The black sheep. The one willing to take the road less traveled to be the change, break generational curses, and build generational wealth! All it takes is one person, right? Congratulations, you've just been inducted into a cult. Don't worry, I too have been a victim of this play on my desire to succeed. The questions you should ask yourself is can I create generational wealth without the buy-in from the present and future generations? What kind of personal wealth do I need to create for myself first? How exactly do I define wealth, and is that definition consistent with the generations I want to supply? While getting the ball rolling in the direction of a generational build is absolutely possible, the likelihood in doing so on your own is very low.

Furthermore, the selling point on any product or service being "generational wealth" is intellectually dishonest because how can one product, be it a course, program, book, life insurance policy, etc., solve generational conditioning, generational oppression, generational lack of access and exploitation, and generational trauma like a magic pill? Selling the idea of generational wealth without focusing on generational healing is the personal finance "diet pill" the fitness influencers who were already fit or paid to have their body done sell you on to get you to pay to be in their program. If you don't get the desired results, hey, you did it wrong. There is no generational wealth without generational buy-in, and there is no generational buy-in without generational healing.

Capitalism: a Necessary Evil?

I've been part of conversations with high-income-earning employees and entrepreneurs alike who are strong believers in capitalism as a form of economic salvation for Black people. Capitalism provides unrestricted growth potential and thus creates the only viable option for economic growth and closing the wealth gap—or so they think. While aspects of this argument are true, it all but ignores the variables outlined throughout this chapter that ties Western capitalism to a multipronged system that promotes, rather than heals, financial trauma. To be clear, capitalism and entrepreneurship are not one and the same. The purpose of this book is not to condemn capitalism as an economic system or to promote alternative economic systems in its stead. The purpose of this book is however to shine a light on the sources of financial trauma as I've observed, experienced, and studied them and to provide avenues to explore what financial healing looks like. One of those avenues involves calling a thing a thing and assessing the variables that induce guilt, shame, fear, and hopelessness when it comes to navigating your relationship with money.

I believe in private ownership. I believe in the creation of jobs and employment options. I believe in a free market. I am however not oblivious to the fact that Blacks and other minorities are not playing the capitalism game on even footing with white people. Not oblivious to the obstacles present via funding, education, experience, or a 200-year head start provided by the exploitation of free labor from Black bodies. I'm also not oblivious to the fact that Black Americans have tried repeatedly through our resilience to build and create despite those obstacles and have endured the intentional destruction, theft, and neglect of assets and resources despite overcoming impossible odds.

Yes, capitalism feels like the key to our salvation because for so long our bodies, our labor, and our talent have been the capital that has produced riches for nearly everyone else.

Through this lens and the previously mentioned lenses of:

- generational trauma passed on through epigenetics
- the vicarious trauma we observe but didn't directly experience
- the workplace and employment trauma that forces us into economic warfare
- and the trauma of poverty and financial instability

It's not difficult to conclude how feelings of mistrust, doubt, fear, anger, hopelessness, or ambivalence can surface when discussing retirement planning, investing, home ownership, or even something as simple as budgeting. While I believe in the need to fight on, to learn, to apply, to build wealth, I also recognize the reflex of survival and the soul level fatigue that can be present. And now, so can you.

Chapter 6

Family, Societal, and Religious Expectations

Faith, Fear, and Deferred Gratification

Do you remember hearing the phrase "Money is the root of all evil" growing up? I don't remember the first time I heard it, but I do know the phrase almost instinctively. Even with the knowledge that the original quote it comes from says that it's the love of money that's the root of all evil, somehow that saying has been codified and recognized as some internally held truth by people as young as high school—sometimes younger.

I taught a workshop on financial therapy one summer to high school age athletes, and I asked them what their money beliefs were from childhood. One of the athletes told me money was the root of all evil. I asked why, and his response was that you can't serve money and serve God. He implied that somehow money was an entity that could be served, and based on his faith, serving the entity of money was against serving God. As a financial therapist, I believe his response spoke to one of four money scripts developed by Dr. Brad Klontz and widely accepted as a contextual framework in financial therapy known as *money avoidance*. A script rooted in scarcity speaks to feelings of guilt around having money or making money, among other things. I'll spend more time on money scripts in Chapter 8. As someone who is culturally and energetically informed, however, his statement and age gave me pause. Money may not be the root of evil, but it does exist within our energy field. The ideas and beliefs we have around money shape its energetic signature in our lives. If we worship, idolize, and otherwise give it power, it will have power over us that is reflected in how we use it and pursue it. Inversely, however, if we heal our relationship with money psychologically, physiologically, and energetically, money will serve us, and our interactions with money, including the ways in which we pursue it, will reflect that.

Hustle culture teaches you that your value is somehow diminished if you are not constantly working and producing. If you do not suffer, struggle, and sacrifice, you are undeserving. A symptom of capitalism, this is also reinforced in the weaponization of religion as a driver to defer enjoying the fruit of your labor into the afterlife despite watching the wealthy elite enjoy their fruits now. This is especially true for Black Americans but echoed throughout the world's marginalized populations including poor white people. Through popular culture you learn to associate a focus on wealth building with a lack of morality or compassion. Caricatures like that of Ebenezer Scrooge from Charles Dickens's *A Christmas Carol* are introduced in childhood portrayed as greedy, selfish, and uncompromising until they hit a redemptive arc that makes them generous due to some loss, illness, or threat to their well-being. If you stop to think about it, how many portrayals of the wealthy capitalist are ever wholly positive? There aren't many if any at all. This subliminally suggests that to get ahead you have to be ruthless, guarded, mean even, and for the onlookers whose values don't align with that, they develop a disdain for those who do.

There's nothing evil or morally wrong with acquiring or possessing money, just as there is nothing good or morally correct about suffering as a virtue. Stuck in between a socialized disdain for poor people and an internal conflict on the issue of building wealth, you exist in this Goldilocks in-between state, making just enough to get by and maybe enjoy your creature comforts but not so much as to become Scrooge. This is the workings of a system designed to keep you dependent on it because without you, it does not work.

The leveraging of religion to reinforce these systems is nothing new and is a noteworthy point to observe. Religious expansion and conflict is almost always accompanied by dollar signs. History shows us accounts of varied religious conquests including the Crusades of the Middle Ages, Constantine's rise to power in Rome, Missionary expansion and Colonialism around the world, Islamic Sharia, separation of Church and State in the U.S. constitution, Chinese Communists' expulsion of Western Missionaries, the Salem Witch trials, up through present-day conflicts in the Gaza Strip.

It's no surprise then that Christianity was not only used to justify slavery in the United States but as a control system to socially engineer compliance of the enslaved. When we hear things like "money is the root of all evil," would it be unreasonable to suspect that perhaps it was an intentional misquote passed on through the generations from the time of slavery? Could it be that Blacks were taught to fear the accumulation of wealth in order to be good slaves and to view their masters' accumulation of wealth as a noble sacrifice made for their salvation? It wasn't long ago that drapetomania was a proposed mental illness that caused enslaved Black people to attempt to flee captivity.[1]

"Black churches were one of the first tools slave masters used to socially engineer Black people...Christianity was used to benefit the White masters...to encourage slaves to

---

[1] Drapetomania was a proposed mental illness by American physician Samuel A. Cartwright.

be 'Christ-like,' render them submissive, justify Black bondage, and instill internal controls over the hearts and minds
of Black slaves." (Anderson, 2001)

This is not an indictment of Christianity.

It's an illustration of how religious systems have been used to
influence our perceptions and interactions with money. To some,
faith is what they have instead of dollars to combat nervous system
dysregulation, and that faith sometimes reinforces harmful associations and narratives about the role of money and how to use it,
deferred long-term planning, and excessive giving that become
values that keep them in a monetary limbo on Earth with claims
of fortunes in the afterlife. But if you do happen to slip through the
cracks and achieve some level of financial success, the back-up plan
to bondage is isolation.

Throughout this section and future sections of the book, I'm
going to encourage the building of community as not only a
resource but a healing mechanism for dealing with financial
trauma. There are few communities I know that are more tight-
knit and committed than the church community. However, we
need to call out not only the way religious institutions have been
weaponized to socially engineer Black people into submissive
and compliant states mentally and emotionally but also financially. The archetype of the God-fearing grandmother tithing her
last dollar rather than paying her light bill because "God got it"
is the kind of perpetuation of financial trauma that plagues our
communities. While tithing in and of itself is a touchy subject for
financial professionals to advise on when brought up against discretionary spending in the face of debt or tight margins on lifestyle expenses, it is a variable that needs to be addressed tactfully
if the practice is causing undue financial harm.

The Myth of Individualism

When you hear the phrase "It's lonely at the top," what immediate feeling do you register? Is it a fire and passion to go and

outwork the competition? Is it anxiety or fear of being alone? Do you think of an exclusive list of people who will get to benefit from your having made it? The truth of the matter is, it's only lonely at the top because you're not supposed to be there alone.

Let's let that statement breathe for a moment.

Society feigns the idea of a meritocracy, where your individual efforts get you individual results. If you work harder than everyone in the room, work while they are sleeping, and take no days off, you're hailed as better, more focused, and more accomplished. Let me be clear—I'm not knocking the high-performing, 5 a.m. club. Focus, discipline, and intentional routines can be powerful tools. But I am asking: who taught you that exhaustion is the price of success? And what are you running from—or toward—when you treat burnout as a badge of honor?

Sometimes it's needed, it's necessary, but it's not because you were designed that way. It's because if you don't have it, you may be left behind in a world where everyone is racing to beat you—and others—to the finish line. What happens when you get to that finish line, though? Do you stop and celebrate? Do you run a new race? Is there even a finish line?

The myth of individualism tells you simultaneously that there will never be enough and that you have to keep going until it is.

The American Dream is an illusion of success.

It plays to your vanity and ego while slowly isolating you from community. Many times its pursuit is in direct opposition to familial cultural values and expectations creating conflict within the high-performance employee or entrepreneur. *"In the African American community, relationship frequently trumps everything else..."* (DeGruy, 2005).

Dr. Joy DeGruy reminds us that **relationship is not weakness—it's cultural strength**. It's our root system. So when we feel that "success" means separation, what we're left with is a cultural dissonance. Due to the communal nature of humans, however, you may find yourself building community within organizations and social clubs based on how you can exploit one another or on the shared premise of making money. This is often referred to as *networking*. You may not like these people but trick yourself into tolerating their presence and engaging with them due to their proximity or because it's socially acceptable. You might find yourself slowly gravitating away from the people who actually know you such as friends you grew up with, family, and members in your community because they don't understand. I'm not talking about the trauma bonded relationships you outgrow in this instance. I'm talking about true friends. You might miss out on family gatherings, milestone events, or casual catch-ups because you're focused on what it takes to get to the next level. You justify this as a necessary and temporary sacrifice as you embed yourself deeper into a culture of workaholism. When you do get a chance to rest, you might be so exhausted you just want to be alone, further isolating yourself. While this may not be true in every instance, what I've just laid out is not a hypothetical scenario. This exact pattern is something both I and the clients I've worked with have experienced.

I had a client once who was a woman. She came from a southeast Asian familial and cultural background and expected to be married off and never in control of her own money. When her family arrived in the United States and she completed her academic studies, she entered the finance industry and suddenly was making more money than even the men in her family. This created some cultural discomfort as women typically didn't take breadwinning roles in her culture. She felt that certainly her father would be a better manager of money than she was, and she added him to her bank account as a co-owner. She quickly realized, however, that this was not true and that he was mismanaging the money, leaving her feeling conflicted. When we met, I had a conversation with her about the tie-in between her personal goals and her values both personally and culturally. She wanted to embrace the independence her peers modeled—but feared becoming alienated from her family in the process.

I didn't encourage her in any one direction or another but rather reminded her of her power to choose in this instance. "You are the boss of your life," I told her, and we began to do an exercise on establishing financial boundaries (discussed in Chapter 13) after which she reportedly felt better.

Why is this important? I believe that you can establish a happy medium where you can both be culturally engaged and establish and maintain financial boundaries in order to best position yourself as an individual and as a member of your community at the same time. However, to do so, you need to abandon the myth of individualism and embrace building community not only as an anchoring mechanism but as a tool for financial healing.

> "It is minority groups that are hurt by the concept of individualism in a society in which wealth and power follow the numbers." (Anderson, 2001)

Sometimes, though, the community you are born into—family especially—can be toxic. They can exhibit toxic patterns and behaviors—traumas—that have been passed down through generations like we talked about in Chapter 1. There can be a social engineering aspect to the culture that the community has adopted or upholds that didn't start with them, and therefore they can't exactly pinpoint why they perpetuate it. You may be in total disagreement with cultural norms, and that is okay. You get to help redefine culture and what it looks like without abandoning family or community.

Milestone Pressure and Identity Debt

Culture is a weapon.

It can be crafted and used against you, or you can wield and define it to the benefit of those who partake in it. Culture usually refers to the norms or systems of behavior and shared values that are passed on from one generation to another (Anderson, 2001, p. 35).

When your relationship with money informs, rather than is informed by, culture, certain expectations and timelines may differ. You may accomplish things like getting married and having children later in life rather than sooner. You might make it a priority to buy a home or invest early. How you prioritize financial milestones may look and feel different from your immediate circle, or it might be exactly the same. My parents were teenagers when I was born. My mother was born to a teenage mother herself. My immediate younger brother was a teenager when his son was born. There was a certain level of dysfunction that came with having teenage parents that I did not want to impart onto my children, so I delayed having any myself, effectively shifting what had become a cultural norm. Choosing not to have children early meant I could use money in my 20s and 30s almost entirely on myself. This included experiences, investments, travel, and buying a home before 30. The point of my sharing this is not to say that my path was a better path than my brother or parents; it's to say that it was an intentional path based on a variety of factors that included the culture of money within my family.

How does or has the culture of money in your family influenced your financial decisions?

This question can be particularly poignant if you are a first-generation wealth builder making a higher income than your parents and other members of your community because there can be a sense of guilt or shame associated with achieving that level of financial success. A survivor's remorse of sorts that some of my clients have reported is often accompanied by feelings of imposter syndrome or luck related to their circumstances despite how hard they've had to work to get there. That's the dilemma of individualism. You view your accomplishments as your own and separate from your born or chosen community thus alienating you when you reap the benefits of their sacrifice. Being disconnected can make you feel less than, alone, or even resentful because of how you perceive your obligations to that community as a task or burden rather than a contribution. These feelings of unease, while internal, may also come from racist socializations explained by Dr. DeGruy as evidenced by the limiting of aspirations in the cases of Black children where they seek out careers as nurses and paralegals rather than as doctors and lawyers (DeGruy, 2005, p. 180). That is to say, because Black children are socialized with inferior ideals or low-bar standards for success, when success is achieved, it feels awkward or unexpected. When simply graduating high school is viewed as the peak accomplishment, or success is measured in your athleticism or ability to entertain, becoming an engineer or doctor feels unattainable. Again, that is culture being used as a weapon. That is also a reaction to systemic exclusion born into a survival strategy. It's not an excuse; it's an explanation. She also points out that racist socialization can be seen when we use the accumulation of material things as the measure of self-worth and success, which speaks to another money script known as money status (Klontz et al., 2015).

Culture, however, is not just limited to language, religious affiliation, ethnicity, or family. When you broaden your perspective of culture to include your place of employment, social groups outside of your family, online media (including TV, social media, radio, movies), status quo or normalized spending patterns associated with holidays or society based expectations, etc., and you observe culture through the lens of it being a weapon, you can take more intentional actions around how you contribute to, participate in, or define culture for yourself. This is your defense against allowing culture to be dictated to you without respect to your unique experiences, background, and aspirations. When you define culture, particularly the culture of money, you get to offer up that definition for others to observe and take part in as well.

It's no wonder so many six-figure earners live paycheck to paycheck while combating inflationary lifestyle expenses. It's the culture of money we've been given that promotes consumerism. If you don't have a plan for your money, someone else does, and that plan likely predates you. Consumerism drives cap-italism, so there will never be a shortage of things or experiences to spend your money on. This pressure to constantly spend is systemic, as we've discussed in the previous chapter. It's not always due to a lack of financial discipline or education. In fact, sometimes it's weaponized financial education that prompts you to spend more by investing in products and services you have no business investing in. Some of my clients, despite having a high income and some basis of financial knowledge, have reported feelings of being behind despite what they've accomplished per-sonally and professionally. They struggle with the idea of what enough is or means to them. This is due to a combination of factors that include a mismatch in values and goals, constantly comparing their journey to the journey of others, and a lack of financial boundary setting. Financial boundary setting doesn't just look like telling others no when they ask for money. Financial boundary setting can also include telling yourself no when eve-rything and everyone is pointing to you needing the next big thing. Yes, I'm going to use the infamous B word here and men-tion a budget, albeit briefly. Financial boundary setting includes having a budget that manages what comes in and what goes out so you can be intentional and strategic about how you are spend-ing as well as what you might be also giving away.

Many of my high-income clients share similar themes when it comes to their frustrations with their personal financial management.

- They experience survivor's guilt.
- They exist in high-income paycheck-to-paycheck cycles.
- They lack effective financial boundaries.
- They frequently engage in social spending.
- They sometimes feel loneliness in their financial challenges due to having high income and being viewed as the family ATM.

While traditional financial educators would take these frustra-tions as purely a lack of discipline or knowledge, you and I will look at these frustrations through a trauma responsive lens that asks the following question:

"What nervous system reaction am I trying to spend my way out of?"

What is the trigger that causes me to deviate from my goals? What am I programming myself to adopt as a value? Is this something that I want to maintain? Is this something that I want to change?

But what about when other people start spending your money for you? I mean that both literally and figuratively. You've done the work, you've attained a high income, you might be on track to living the lifestyle of your dreams, but that community that I mentioned has their hands out asking you for money while at the same time asking you "what's next?" after every major milestone. Insert the "Black tax."

The Cost of Breaking Through

While not an experience exclusive to Black Americans, the Black tax refers to a practice where a successful Black individual supports members of their immediate and extended family financially (Sabree, 2023). Without established financial boundaries and cultural clarity, the Black tax places a tremendous burden of expectation on first-generation high earners trying to find their financial footing. This contributes to financial anxiety and financial stress that can result in a people pleasing or financial fawning behavior where the individual gives away or feels pressured to use money in a way that may leave them feeling resentful or burdened by the expectation that they have to give in order to be valued, loved, or accepted in their community circles. In Chapter 13 I will outline strategies and approaches that allow you to adhere to your values without overextending yourself financially and how to say no while still contributing to your community.

Money creates access. As you experience greater social mobility because of your financial status, you may encounter experiences that members of your community cannot access or simply don't know exists. Due to this lack of access they may view your access with feelings of envy or disdain. In return, you may struggle with feelings of unease or even guilt because you can't bring them along for the ride. This cultural ripple is a feature of capitalism that is not your fault but one that can, if not named and identified, work to further alienate and isolate you from your community. As I encourage you to lean into your community, create culture, and establish boundaries, I have to emphasize the importance of you building a foundation for yourself financially, physiologically, and socially first. That's what this book aims to solve for and what the later portions of this book will instruct on.

Bonus Perspective: Financial Trauma in Entrepreneurship

In Chapter 4 I briefly described how I left my job in reaction to the workplace and employment trauma I experienced. I decided I could and should become my own boss to experience time freedom, avoid burnout, and improve my mental health. I think I make a compelling argument against toxic workplaces that might inspire people on a particular path to quit their jobs and jump into entrepreneurship for themselves. In sharing my story with the world, I've had so many people reach out to me for advice on how I did it and what I needed to do in order to prepare and even had some people tell me that my going back to work would result in them losing hope. While I offered what I could by way of advice, shared the first annual anniversary of quitting my job on social media, and even started an "I Fired My Boss" brand, I internalized the comment about going back, resulting in lost hope for a stranger I've never met in person on such a deep level that I'm still not sure if my perseverance in entrepreneurship was based solely on the grit I possessed or some self-righteous desire to be a beacon of hope for others on this path. For that reason I wanted to add this bonus perspective to discuss some of the financial trauma that came with my entrepreneurial experience. The money isn't always greener on the other side.

Doing the Most as a Trauma Response

Before quitting my job in May 2021, I started working with a coach to build a digital product—a course—that I was convinced would make me a lot of money. The cost for the coach's service was $5,000 that I put on a business credit card. We worked together to build the course based on the premise that the ideas present in my book *Financially Irresponsible* were monetizable and that with the right packaging and advertising people would buy it at a price point of $297. It was crude, low-budget, and had terrible production value, but I never built a course before and was so full of optimism—and disdain for my current situation at work—that I felt like it had to work. Halfway through the completion of the project, the coach ghosted me, and I was left to figure out the marketing and fulfillment of the product. I started marketing the product with little conversion and was convinced that I needed to get the product in front of more people. I started paying Instagram shoutout pages to promote the course and running my own ads on social media. I had a handful of discounted purchases. I was offering an affiliate split on the course for anyone who sold the course. I also started marketing a 30-day financial coaching program for $1,000. I thought at the time that I could diversify my income with coaching and digital

(continued)

(continued)

product sales. I quit my job soon after and immediately felt the pressure to replace my income. Coincidentally around this time a crafty salesperson disguised as a digital marketer slid into my DMs telling me that they worked for an agency that could get my course to scale with Facebook Ads. They said for every $1 I put into ad spend, I'd get $3 back. I was skeptical, but he got his CEO on the phone, and they made me these outlandish guarantees like if I didn't earn my money back in sales after the first 30 days, they would work with me for free until I did. I swiped my business credit card again for $3,500 emphasizing to the two owners that I need this to work. I have no job and no income, so please don't screw me.

It's okay, you can laugh at me. I was a naive mark and brand new to full-time entrepreneurship. Of course, an additional $3,000 later and $0 in conversions made me not only panic but upset. I began calling and texting every day, yelling at my client success rep about how I could be spending so much money for this proprietary system for sales and getting no conversions. The next thing I knew I was locked out of their system and told I was a difficult customer to work with. I threatened legal action but didn't have the money to follow through. Eventually I found out they sold the agency and exited. Took my money— and probably that of several others—and ran.

Twice in a row I was left hanging. I felt like a sucker.

The lesson? Scarcity marketing also employs a dangerous form of reverse psychology that says if you don't "invest" in yourself, you have a scarcity mindset. There is a difference between betting on yourself and betting on a service someone else is offering under the guise of betting on yourself.[2] As a

[2]See https://x.com/RahkimSabree/status/1454861150601060355.

new entrepreneur, you might feel like you need to spend your way out of your trauma response in the same way you might have as an employee. I know I did. Leaving your job doesn't remove the triggers to trauma that employment might have been pulling. In some cases, it might make those triggers much more apparent. This wasn't just about two bad investments. It was about trying to buy safety. Trying to feel like I was doing something. In hindsight, I wasn't investing in success—I was outsourcing my stability.

Isolation and Identity

After I left corporate, I had become so radicalized in establishing an anti-corporate identity that I did a paid international workshop with my durag[3] on. It was a hit with the audience as we discussed themes of authenticity in the workplace and inclusive business practices. I had all but cut up and burned my collection of ties and dress shirts in my desire to separate myself from the corporate identity I had built for close to a decade. I was tired of code-switching, tired of the dress code, tired of the corporate lingo, and ready to fully lean into this new era of being my own boss. About nine months into my full-time journey, I was still trying to figure out how to make steady income. I did a few 1099 gigs here and there. Some writing, some speaking, some social media strategy, but every day felt like a hunt and hustle. I did have significant savings tied up in investments and access to large credit lines, but I was tapping into those much more frequently than I was okay with. Still, the idea of returning to a "job" felt like a betrayal, not just to myself but to all the people who rallied

(continued)

---

[3]A durag is a hair covering used to tie down long or curly hair.

(continued)

behind me when I made my announcement on social media, traditional media, and even on TV as a guest on Tamron Hall's show. I didn't realize it at the time, but I slowly began to fill the vacuum left by destroying my corporate identity with a new entrepreneurial one. The only problem was I wasn't making enough money. A recruiter contacted me after receiving my information from someone who knew me about a role with a small credit union heading up their marketing team. This would have been the job of my dreams when I was still working, with great pay and visibility. Me and the recruiter hit it off and they were very impressed with my work experience and what I had built for myself since leaving my previous employer. She wanted to move to the next steps in the process. I asked what working for the credit union would mean for my personal brand. If I'd be permitted to continue building my brand without issue because that was ultimately what caused my previous departure.

Her answer? "Due to the visible nature of the role, the company will want you to focus exclusively on their marketing efforts."

I shared that that was a non-negotiable deal breaker for me and that I would have to pass. I turned down a six-figure employment opportunity, and I had a letter in the mail threatening to repossess my car due to nonpayment. I was three months behind.

Immediately I called my father to ask him if I was crazy for what I did. He said, "Son, you might have bigger balls than I do."

In hindsight, I probably should have taken the opportunity, but in that moment I felt the stance I took was not only the right thing to do but that anything contrary would be a betrayal spiritually, mentally, and emotionally. I left corporate

America so that I could experience freedom on my terms. One thing I've learned about freedom is that freedom is not free.

From a trauma responsive perspective, I can see how my nervous system made a dangerous association with the idea of going back to work. It was too soon, and I hadn't given myself the opportunity to succeed just yet. From a purely financial standpoint, it was probably the dumbest money decision I've ever made. One thing, though, is for certain. If I would have taken that job, I would not be writing this book. I would not have secured a column with Forbes or pursued financial therapy or my accreditation as a financial counselor. Making that sacrifice led to the opening of many doors that wouldn't have otherwise been opened. But at least I would have had a job.

That was a burden I had to carry mostly alone. Entrepreneurship looks great on social media, but it's not often discussed through the lens of how isolating it can be. You're in this space of pure ether reconstructing and getting to know your deepest flaws and strengths. You oscillate between wanting to give up entirely and pure determination. You are on a spiritual journey like no other; it's 12 in the afternoon, and everyone you know and want to talk to is at work. You have to tighten your spending, so you decline social invitations and recreational trips to save money. Some of your friends and family understand; others take it personally. You feel like the world is on fire and you're drowning at the same time, but you have to smile and pretend everything is okay because, well, entrepreneurship was a choice, wasn't it? You could go back to work. You could get a job.

Entrepreneurship has been one of the most isolating experiences I've ever had.

(continued)

(continued)

But isolation also gave me room to face myself—and to ask better questions about what I really value. Not just financial freedom, but emotional autonomy. Not just success, but sustainability. Entrepreneurship didn't heal my financial trauma—it exposed it. And in doing so, it gave me the opportunity to finally face it—and write this book.

Author Note: I've created additional resources to accompany this book including videos, micro courses, and more. Scan the following QR code or visit RahkimSabree.com/resources to access them.

Part II

EDUCATION: EXPLORING CONTEXTUAL FRAMEWORKS AND METHODS

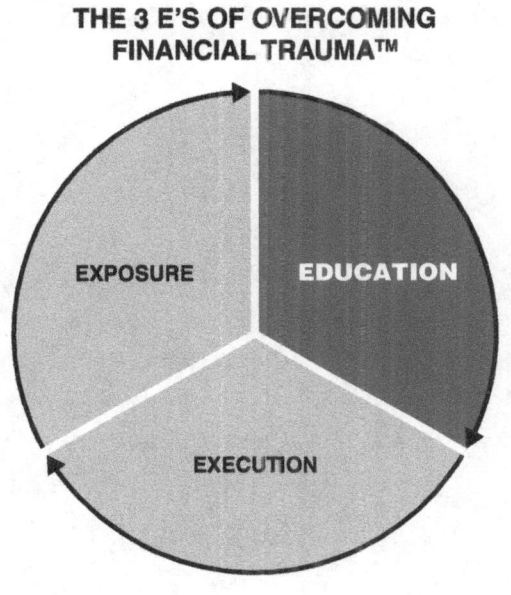

Chapter 7

How Financial Trauma Manifests in the Mind and Body

In the first part of this book, I introduced the vocabulary of financial trauma and explored some of the external forces that shape it. My perspective is rooted in how we react to the systems we navigate—but by now, you might be wondering: what can I actually do about it?

To better understand your responses to financial trauma, it's important to look beyond behavior alone. You need a foundational understanding of how trauma lives in your body—not just in what you do but in how you feel, react, and carry stress.

That means looking at your nervous system, your hormonal patterns, and even your inherited biology. When you experience money, you're not just making decisions—you're having a full-body experience. Financial trauma isn't just emotional. It's physical, mental, and spiritual.

Trauma lives in the body—and so does healing.

The Biology of Safety and Survival

I'm not a mental health professional. My background is in banking and finance. So, what does budgeting or building credit have to do with your nervous system? Honestly, a lot more than I thought.

When I was writing *Financially Irresponsible*, I was also reading Dr. Joy DeGruy's *Post Traumatic Slave Syndrome*. She breaks down intergenerational trauma through the lens of post-traumatic stress and looks at how the trauma from slavery in the United States and Jim Crow didn't just disappear—it was passed down, shaping behavior across generations of Black Americans. That idea stuck with me.

I started thinking about how this same concept could apply to our financial behavior—how our relationship with money could be rooted in survival, in patterns we didn't consciously choose. How much of our financial behavior is just our reactions to the environments we navigate? That's when I first started using the phrase *financial trauma from generational trauma*. I didn't realize at the time that I was stepping into the intersection of two completely different conversations—one about money and one about trauma—that rarely get talked about together.

Most financial literacy content leans heavy on logic, discipline, and numbers—but even heavier on blame and shame. All the "could've, should've, would've but didn't" energy. What if you looked at survival, coping, and stories passed down over time? For me, that was a game changer. Why? Because for a long time, I tried to be *the example*. The one who beat the odds and rose above. I believed—and still believe— in personal empowerment but recognized that that narrative alone leaves out a lot. It ignores the weight of systems, the impact of generational trauma, and the psychological toll of existing in extended or even permanent "survival mode."

As I kept digging, I found myself deep in psychology, neuroscience, therapeutic modalities, and even energy-based frameworks—like those explored in Dr. Joe Dispenza's *Becoming Supernatural*—that connects emotion, belief, and behavioral change to draw parallels between what money represents, how it's used as a tool, and what actually drives financial behavior. That search led me beyond budgeting spreadsheets and credit hacks into the world of financial wellness. Eventually, I found the Financial Therapy Association and the Association for Financial Counseling and Planning Education, where professionals are using evidence-based approaches to close the gap between psychology and money habits.

That experience reignited my already present interest in human behavior—not just what people *do* with money, but *why they* do it. That's when things really started to connect for me: the overlap between systems, wealth, mental health, and race-based trauma. Within these professional groups, my ideas were received as niche, courageous, even pioneering. Revolutionary, someone said, for how my ideas shifted the conversation around money and wellness. I began to get familiar with financial therapy–specific terms like money scripts and money disorders and found myself learning more and more about the clinical approaches to helping people with money.

To unpack all of that, we've got to start with the body—and specifically, the nervous system. Because whether you're swiping a credit card or avoiding a bank statement, your nervous system is already reacting before you make a single conscious choice.

The nervous system is often described as being broken down into three evolutionary parts.

- **The reptilian or animal brain**, existing in the brain stem and responsible for basic bodily functions like breathing, using the bathroom, etc.
- **The mammalian brain or limbic system**, responsible for monitoring danger and acts as the seat of emotions
- **The neocortex**, which is responsible for executive function like language, abstract thought, planning, reflecting, and understanding cause and effect

In the book *The Body Keeps the Score*, Dr. Bessel Van Der Kolk does a great job breaking down the triune brain or three-part description of the brain, citing the neuroscientist Paul Maclean and explaining how trauma and post-traumatic stress disorder can change how the brain operates on a default basis over time. Essentially, he describes the function of the reptilian brain and limbic system as the parts of the brain that look out for your welfare. The amygdala, existing in the limbic system, acts as a sensor that sorts through our experiences and sensations to determine if they are relevant for survival. If a threat is perceived, it automatically triggers the autonomic nervous system and stress hormones to create a body response.

If you've ever experienced a layoff, missed a payment, received a phone call from a bill collector, been denied credit, or didn't have money on hand for a financial emergency, you're likely familiar with this body response. You might describe the associated feeling as dread, panic, embarrassment, or anxiety, but your amygdala sees threat and automatically enlists the help of your bodily functions and hormones, like cortisol and adrenaline, to prepare you to do whatever is necessary to achieve safety. These responses are often referred to as fight or flight responses.

The frontal lobe, specifically the prefrontal cortex, existing in the neocortex, sits higher in the brain than the amygdala and is the youngest evolutionary part of the brain. In situations where the amygdala automatically detects a threat without judgment, the prefrontal cortex will regulate emotion, restore balance, and abort the stress response if it determines there is a false alarm. Essentially, the prefrontal cortex is that friend who acts as the voice of reason when you are upset and about to act on that emotion.

What I found interesting about these parts of the brain is that while they generally work in harmony with one another, they are capable of acting independently of each other, especially when it comes to matters of survival. This explains how financial stress can exist in perpetuity while administrative control in other parts of your life may seem normal. While the triune brain model is widely used as a teaching framework, there's some debate around whether it oversimplifies the complexity of the brain. So think of this as a conceptual map—not a literal blueprint. The goal here isn't scientific perfection, but to better understand how trauma impacts behavior, especially in the context of money. It's like an ever-present smoke alarm beep becoming the background noise; your amygdala is recognizing financial trauma as danger, but your prefrontal cortex sees a false alarm until the alarm feels like background noise. As I write this, I became conscious of the fact that my own smoke alarm's consistent chirp has been letting me know it needs new batteries, yet I've allowed this constant alert to become background noise much in the same way I'm describing.

Your dealings with money on the surface—like checking your bank account, paying a bill, or creating a budget—may trigger a trauma response. These moments often connect to personal, lived experiences that your nervous system has stored as threats. Viewed through the traditional, siloed personal finance lens, this places the blame squarely on the individual. It gets framed as a lack of discipline, a scarcity mindset, or poor money habits.

But now you know that these experiences don't always reflect good or bad decisions—they reflect your nervous system's perception of danger. That perception is shaped not just by personal experience but by what money represents to you: safety, survival, power, shame, etc. And often, it is shaped by the social contracts we're forced into—systems built around inequality, control, and access.

When financial stress hits, your brain doesn't just process numbers—it processes risk. More often than not that stress comes from circumstances outside of your control, the systems and variables I outlined in Part I of this book. When that risk feels high enough, it triggers your body's survival response. In the next section, I'll break down how those trauma responses—fight, flight, freeze, and fawn—show up in your financial behavior.

Author Note: I've created additional resources to accompany this book including videos, micro courses, and more. Scan the following QR code or visit RahkimSabree.com/resources to access them.

Trauma Responses: Fight, Flight, Freeze, Fawn

When I started my own financial journey, I remember the sense of pride I held in what I accomplished. I also remember making some disparaging statements online about Black people on their own financial journeys, specifically related to having food stamps and Section 8.

> "Black people need to get away from this "section 8" mentality. You are better than the benefits dangled in your face that forces your men out of the house and onto child support & that keeps you from earning an income so that you can qualify for food stamps and welfare."

I meant well, but imagine that. Me, a product of Section 8, making such an inflammatory and insensitive statement on a public forum. The issue was that I experienced a little bit of upward social mobility and learned a few financial concepts that made me feel a bit uppity. In the process of trying to encourage and elevate people who looked like me to perform as I did, it escaped me that the issues that afflict them are not so easily swayed by a magic wand or deciding to do better. While making that decision is a key step in the process, there are almost always other variables at play, and one of the main variables is that of focusing simply on survival. Viewed from an isolated lens, what manifests as financial trauma feels like a personal failure and thus perceived attacks to the ways in which you learn to cope with that trauma also feel threatening. When examining the effects of trauma transmitted through generations, Dr. DeGruy has this to say: "How do we learn to raise our children? Almost entirely through our own experience of being raised. Of course there are things our parents did that we decide we'll do differently, but for the most part parenting is one of a myriad of skills that is passed down generation to generation." If that trauma is money related, would it not then also be the case that you learn from how you were raised? From what you observed?

So you might decide to work harder, longer hours, and multiple jobs, sacrificing sleep and your physical health in a fight response. The bills are getting paid, but you're living paycheck to paycheck having to juggle what gets paid and when. The bills that don't get paid start piling up, so you avoid them and start ignoring phone calls or refusing to open mail in a flee response. Prioritizing survival over anything else, you may or may not qualify for assistance in the form of food stamps or housing vouchers. You experience temporary relief but are so far in the arrears you don't know what to address first. You freeze. Psychologists Martin Seligman and Steven Maier call this learned helplessness.[1] In their research, dogs with repeated exposure to electric shocks in a locked cage come to believe that no amount of effort will make a difference even after the cage doors are unlocked. Finally, the dogs are free, but their circumstances have trained them to both endure the discomfort of the shocks and believe that efforts to escape don't matter. This freeze response isn't laziness or weakness. It's a survival strategy in response not only to the trauma you've experienced in your lifetime but the trauma you've inherited from generations prior. Patterns of avoidance, disconnection, workaholism, and hypervigilance can look like bad habits, but they are physiological and automatic responses to the real or imagined threat present when dealing with both a lack and abundance of money.

---

[1]This is referencing this study "Failure to escape traumatic shock," Seligman, M. E., & Maier, S. F. (1967). Failure to escape traumatic shock. *Journal of Experimental Psychology*, 74(1), 1–9. https://doi.org/10.1037/h0024514

Response	How It Shows Up Financially	What It Might Look Like
Fight	Overworking, arguing over money, obsessing over control	Hustling nonstop, debating bills, trying to "conquer" scarcity
Flight	Avoiding bills, ghosting financial tasks, changing jobs often	Ignoring account balances, dodging calls, abandoning budgets
Freeze	Feeling stuck, overwhelmed, paralyzed by decisions	Unopened mail, procrastinating on basic tasks, inaction
Fawn	Over-giving, people-pleasing with money, lacking boundaries	Loaning money you don't have, co-signing under pressure, avoiding conflict

THE TRIUNE BRAIN FRAMEWORK

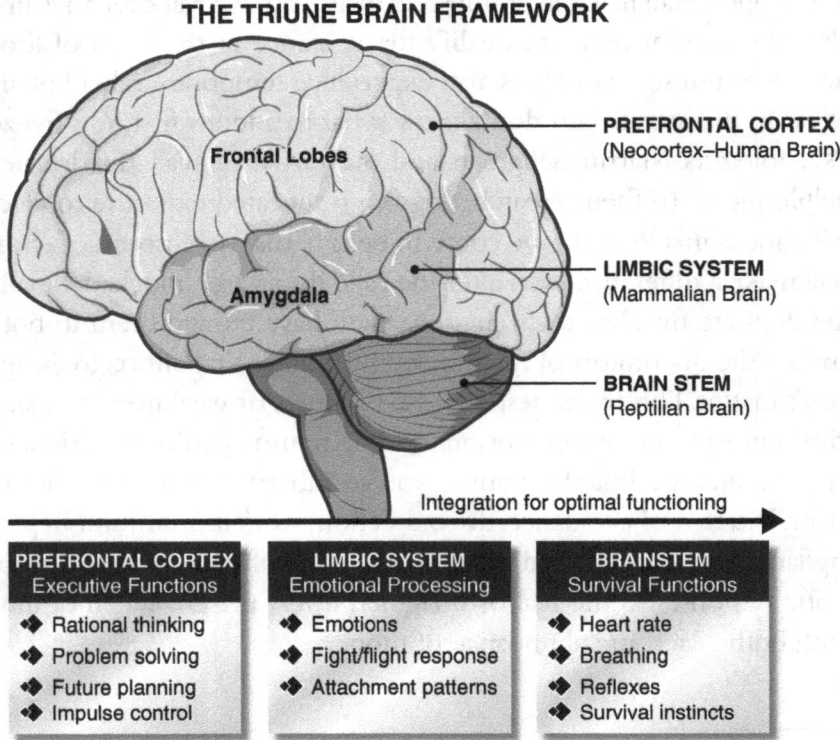

Frontal Lobes

PREFRONTAL CORTEX
(Neocortex–Human Brain)

Amygdala

LIMBIC SYSTEM
(Mammalian Brain)

BRAIN STEM
(Reptilian Brain)

Integration for optimal functioning

PREFRONTAL CORTEX Executive Functions	LIMBIC SYSTEM Emotional Processing	BRAINSTEM Survival Functions
❖ Rational thinking	❖ Emotions	❖ Heart rate
❖ Problem solving	❖ Fight/flight response	❖ Breathing
❖ Future planning	❖ Attachment patterns	❖ Reflexes
❖ Impulse control		❖ Survival instincts

DEVELOPMENTAL SEQUENCE

Brain stem (birth) → Limbic (early childhood) → Prefrontal Cortex (adolescence = 25 years)

Illustration based on the Triune Brain Theory developed and popularized by Paul D. MacLean

Epigenetics and Generational Transfer

When I began to be recognized as a financial educator, the number-one question I received—and sometimes still get—was "what should I invest in?" I turned it into a joke. I believed in the notion that if you give a man a fish, he eats for a day, but if you teach a man to fish, he eats for a lifetime. I wanted to teach people how to fish financially, not serve up answers on a platter. Furthermore, I wasn't licensed to give that kind of advice, so to the dismay of the people asking, I stayed away from telling them what to invest in and instead educate them on how to invest. I was an educator after all. While a case can be made for intellectual laziness in that the people asking just didn't want to do the work to determine what to invest in, a trauma responsive lens could acknowledge that these people didn't trust themselves to make the decision. More than that, they truly distrusted the financial system they were opting into but, pushed to the edges of discomfort, recognized that major wealth creation was made on the stock market and they wanted a piece of that action; they believed they *needed* to be there. What I didn't recognize then was that maybe their apprehension and their distrust was a warranted echo of previous generational trauma that they were unconsciously trying to cut through. Maybe their method of circumventing that trauma was to trust the professional who was friendly, seemed to know more than they did, and looked like them. Of course, back then I believed as most new financial educators believe. That financial literacy and a bit of a mindset shift would solve systemic barriers from generations past and present day. That if you know better, you do better. Today I recognize that this was wrong.

I touched on epigenetics in the first chapter briefly, but here I want to give you the science. Epigenetics is the study of how life experiences can alter the expression of your genes. This doesn't change your genes themselves, just how they are expressed. These experiences include traumatic ones that can affect not only the people who live through them but the genes of their children and even their grandchildren. "From *The Body Keeps the Score*, Life events can trigger biochemical messages that turn genes on or off . . . Methylation patterns, however, can be passed on to offspring—a phenomenon known as epigenetics."

How you react to money is not only based on the trauma responses you have from your lived experiences but also the response to trauma from your parents and grandparents. Before the study of epigenetics became mainstream, Canadian psychiatrist Vivian Rakoff and colleagues documented their suspicions around trauma experienced from Holocaust survivors transferring to their children. This became the foundation for what Dr. Rachel Yehuda would later confirm in her epigenetics research. That trauma can be passed down biologically, not just through learned behavior. When systems have been successful in the exploitation of people (capitalism), trusting those systems becomes a risk factor in your survival. When examinations of the numbers related to Black homeownership as an example or Black investors in the stock market are showcased, often the call to action is *more* financial education. Greater access to programs that lower the barrier to entry for Black people to purchase property to begin with. What if the shadow barrier to Black ownership is not educational but physiological? What if Black people have an aversion to ownership due to unreconciled pain from a time when their direct ancestors were considered property?

> "Another fairly common traumatic retention is a reticence to own a home or a business. . .It's not hard to see how people whose ancestors were considered property would not be delighted by the concept of ownership" (Menakem, 2017).

Dr. Yehuda's work with descendants of Holocaust survivors revealed measurable changes in stress hormone regulation passed down from one generation to the next. As we examine the events of slavery that act as the foundation for wealth building in the United States, and its legacy that built institutions like J.P. Morgan Bank, and stand it next to the behavior of marginalized people around the accumulation of material things as the measure of self-worth and success, suddenly that "irresponsible" behavior makes sense. "Black are the only group of people forced to practice capitalism without capital in the richest and most capitalistic nation on earth" (Anderson, 2001).

Dr. Claud Anderson's work shows how law, monopolies, and land were systematically layered to disadvantage Black Americans. Epigenetics research demonstrates that the legacies of systems have caused protracted trauma, resulting in a financially disempowered and traumatized population that continues to react as a whole through the lens of trauma and survival responses even when it comes to money management.

One of my favorite stories to tell is how every year from my late teens until I turned 30 my dad would reflect on where he was in age the year I was born and where I was when I got to the same age. He would tell me that he didn't envision living to 30 himself and that to see me reach 30 was not only a blessing, but the breaking of a generational curse. Why? Because despite the traumas he lived through, and the traumas his father lived through, I've never once considered the possibility that I would not live to 30, and to him, that was a marked improvement in our family bloodline. Imagine thinking you won't live beyond 30? How then do you conceptualize long-term financial planning like retirement or buy and hold investing? The sad part is, my dad is not the only person who thought this way.

When considering the ideas around wealth accumulation and wealth transfer for yourself and your family, it's important to take into account your family's generational trauma and generational survival tactics that show up not just in your financial decisions but also in your diet, your environment, and overall physical and spiritual health.

Repeat after me: I will no longer shame my survival. My body has been protecting me—and now I choose to listen, not judge.

Chapter 8

Understanding Financial Avoidance and Shame

What Is Money Shame

In Chapter 2 I briefly reference a memory from elementary school where my classmates and I participated in a Scholastic book fair and school trips with gift shops I didn't have the money to spend in. I mention that I found common ground with the classmates who didn't have money to purchase anything either, but I didn't mention what feelings came with sitting to the side as a sort of social outcast while all the students with money from their parents were able to buy various gifts, school supplies, books, or toys that I wanted. This feeling became a familiar feeling throughout my childhood. When all the kids had the Yomega Fireball Yo-yo, I had some secondary no-name yo-yo. When the popular Razor scooter came out, I got a gold and black Schwinn "Sting-Ray" scooter. I was a grateful child, and name brands were never really my thing, but I do remember the looks, the snickers, the laughs, and the comments made about how my parents couldn't afford to get me the popular brands of these items that worked exactly the same way as the less popular ones. The feeling

I'm referring to was money shame, and I can trace my first feelings of money-related shame back to about the age of 7.

What's interesting about that age of 7 is that there is an often quoted study from 2013 titled "Habit formation and learning in young children" where it's implied that children's habits around money surface as early as 7 (Whitebread & Bingham, 2013). While there is some intellectual debate around whether or not those habits become fixed or act as a foundation for later money beliefs in adulthood, I certainly remember those feelings of money shame and how that shame has contributed to the money scripts I've adopted over the years.

Money shame is the feeling of humiliation or distress related to your financial circumstances. As a child, these circumstances exist largely outside of your control, which can trigger one of the four body responses I discussed in the previous chapter: fight, flight, freeze, fawn. As an adult, however, we have more power to adjust our discomfort due to money shame than we did as children ironically by using or avoiding money. I'll share more on money avoidance in a bit, but some of the common sources of money shame I see include:

- Debt
- Financial decisions
- Societal comparisons
- Cultural taboos
- And financial educators/service providers

That list is pretty intuitive, but I do want to spend some time discussing financial decisions and the financial service provider bullet points. In a workshop I run on money shame, I break down the sources of money shame similar to the way I just did here. The bullet point on financial decisions used to read "*poor* financial decisions" until one day I stopped myself midway through the workshop and corrected my language. The thing is, while it would be easy for me as a financial educator or service provider to point the finger at someone's financial decisions and say that was a bad decision, the truth is people generally don't want to make a poor financial decision. That decision more often than not felt like the best decision to make at that moment. Maybe in hindsight you learn from the decision and decide you'll never do it again. Maybe you didn't want to make that decision in the first place but felt like you didn't have a choice. Maybe your motivations and influences in making that decision were coming from a place of informed consent where you felt the need to self-soothe financially was greater than the negative outcome from your decision. In all of these instances you might experience money shame due to the outcome of your decision or the factors that prompted the decision and not necessarily the decision itself.

You are the expert on your life.

For that reason I include financial service providers as a common source of money shame. Financial services specifically and personal finance broadly by and large has placed the blame on the individual rather than the systems individuals are reacting to. Many times, financial educators—credentialed and uncredentialed—act as agents of the system exploiting people for profit. We don't always realize we're doing it, and sometimes we are tied down by compliance, regulations, and the culture of financial advisory that uses coded language to shame or guilt you into a product, service, or behavior we can later monetize. Part of our role is to teach you how to navigate an exploitative system within our area of specialization in a "done for you, done with you, or teach you how to do it yourself" model.

That's not to say all or even most financial services providers are bad or malicious. There are a growing number of us who are waking up to holistic financial wellness strategies to implement with our clients so that we are acknowledging the whole person and their circumstances outside of the silo of finance. When I teach financial service providers, corporate and nonprofit leaders, and HR professionals about financial shame and subsequent (or previous) financial trauma, I have to center the end user. I center you in the conversation. Again, you are the expert on your life.

Trauma viewed through a post-traumatic stress disorder (PTSD) lens is often categorized in the categories of "Big T" and "little t" trauma, with the main differentiator being that "Big T" trauma poses a threat to one's physical safety, sense of survival, or emotional integrity. Applied to financial trauma, these would be your flash-point financial experiences, the clinically accepted definition of financial trauma often referred to. While financially traumatic situations like experiencing poverty, bankruptcy, homelessness, divorce, and others can certainly bring on a PTSD-like response, that doesn't minimize the impact of "little t" trauma scenarios including vicarious trauma, workplace trauma, cultural taboos, living paycheck to paycheck, or a retail therapy shame cycle. Because these scenarios are often not viewed through a neurobiological or behavioral lens, these constant mini-threats can induce the production of cortisol, a stress hormone, without being noticed or acknowledged. While you may not recognize that your nervous system is reacting to a perceived threat due to socialized beliefs that "little t" financial trauma falls under normal behavior, your nervous system still reacts and adapts to it.

It's important to point out here that the pervasive impact of financial trauma whether it's considered "Big T" or "little t" trauma affects not only nervous system regulation but subsequent behaviors and beliefs about money as well.

Understanding Financial Trauma

"Big T" Trauma	"Little t" Trauma
◆ Poverty	◆ Parents fighting about money
◆ Hunger	◆ Parents stressed about money
◆ Vulnerability to crime	◆ Living paycheck to paycheck
◆ Great Recession/COVID	◆ Retail therapy shame cycle
◆ Bankruptcy	◆ Money taboo
◆ Divorce	◆ Workaholism
◆ Foreclosure	◆ Toxic work culture
◆ Homelessness	◆ Inter-generational financial support
◆ Theft/robbery	
◆ Unemployment	

The Impact of Money Shame

Money shame results in emotional distress that can lead to avoidance behaviors and secrecy. You may ask yourself questions like, am I not good enough, or a series of "why can't I" questions.

- Why can't I make more money?
- Why can't I achieve my goals?
- Why can't I provide for my family?

That shame can trigger a cycle of money avoidance shown in the following diagram, where your shame results in an avoidant behavior that then results in a negative financial consequence and increased shame or trauma.

The Cycle of Money Avoidance

- Financial Stressor
- Emotional Response (Shame/Trauma)

- Negative Financial Consequences
- Increased Shame and Trauma

Avoidance Behavior

Financial shame and trauma lead to avoidance, which results in neglecting financial responsibilities and worsening the situation.

Financial avoidance can look like procrastination, like not checking accounts, not opening mail, screening phone calls for bill collectors, and not doing your taxes. It can look like hypervigilance and workaholism by trying to distract yourself from the feelings of shame tied to either your financial circumstances or your behavior. Financial avoidance can also look like overspending. To cope, people try to shut themselves down and develop tunnel vision and hyperfocus. If they can't shut down naturally, they may enlist drugs or alcohol to block out the world (Van Der Kolk, 2015, pp. 70–71). You may use your money to avoid dealing with deeply held beliefs or responses to financial circumstances. Buying drinks during happy hour, gambling and sports betting, retail therapy, and paying for pornography can be considered avoidant tactics. Even tithing can be an avoidant strategy. I mention tithing briefly in Chapter 6 but don't spend time unpacking the motivations behind tithing; the practice itself can come from an attempt to soothe or altogether avoid financial trauma. While it can be a deeply affirming and aligning spiritual practice, tithing can also be driven by shame, guilt, or desperation (see also: *zakat* in Islam). Shame-based giving certainly falls into the cycle of money avoidance as shame is being instituted as the premise for financial behavior. Additionally, individuals may tithe as a demonstration of faith despite their circumstances, opting rather to contribute to their church or religious centers as a form of sacrificial obedience than to address areas in their financial picture they have the ability to work on changing.

The idea here is not exclusively that you are using money to avoid a money issue but that you are using money to find ways to cope with some dysregulation in your nervous system in a way that may be harmful to your financial goals or circumstances. Due to the nature of consumerism culture, your nervous system is constantly being manipulated with advertisements and marketing, like we discussed in Chapter 5, to cause this exact reaction. That's not to say you shouldn't use your money for things and experiences you enjoy but rather that you should examine how and why you use money and what you are trying to spend your way out of. Sometimes money avoidance is more than just a nervous system reaction and more so a deeply held belief.

> **Reflection questions:**
> - What's one memory where you felt ashamed of money growing up?
> - What behavior do you repeat that you know is rooted in money shame?
> - When do you most avoid looking at your finances—and why?

Money Scripts

When I first encountered the topic of money scripts, a term coined by Dr. Brad Klontz, I spent so much time thinking about not only my own money script, but the money scripts of other people. I would hear someone share a thought or reflection related to money and would immediately try to categorize what their dominant money script might be. This was good practice in understanding and identifying the four common money scripts but not so much in terms of labeling and classifying people as if their beliefs about money were criteria for a diagnosis. Introduction to money scripts should be approached as a contextual framework for how beliefs about money may influence or be reflected in money behaviors.

Money scripts are underlying assumptions or beliefs about money that are typically only partially true, are often developed in childhood, and are unconsciously followed throughout adulthood (Klontz et al., 2015). While money scripts are largely subjective and vary into the hundreds, financial therapy recognizes four primary money scripts that can act as indicators to predict money disorders. The four money scripts are:

- Money avoidance
- Money worship
- Money status
- Money vigilance

Money avoidance according to Klontz is characterized by systematically avoiding dealing with your money while rejecting personal responsibility for your financial health. You might deal with fear, disgust, or anxiety when it comes to money and associate negative feelings with money such as money is the root of all evil, that wealthy people are greedy, and that you are better off without money.

While I believe the money avoidance script to be prevalent within the Black and adjacent minority communities, I think it's important to contextualize that script through the lens of marginalization, institutional traumas, and lived experience. The money avoidance script is reflective of a capitalist influence, and those feelings of fear, disgust, or anxiety are warranted if you are part of the working class. While much of this book is a critique of the systems we navigate inclusive of capitalism, it is not a critique of you navigating the system in the ways that are advantageous to you. The idea of accepting personal responsibility for your financial health in this instance means you must be engaged in the practice of *financial advancement* to the extent that it strikes a healthy balance in how you view and use money. Financial advancement simply means you are actively taking steps to be personally responsible and accountable for your financial health. It's like the idea of radical accountability applied to money. It's not my fault, but, yes it is. No one is going to save you, and even if someone does throw you a life raft, you've got to be the one to decide to get on it.

Money worship is characterized by the belief that if you had more money, you would be happier. Workaholism and hoarding money are common behaviors associated with this money script, and people with this money script may make associations between money and safety, happiness, power, and displays of love.

If you're reading this book, I imagine the money worship script is a dominant money script you have; I know it is for me. In fact, due to my upbringing, I largely believed that my dominant money script was money avoidance until I took the Klontz

Money Script® Inventory Revised (KMSI-R) and found that I scored highest on money worship.[1] This makes sense contextually because as an entrepreneur I do make associations between success and security with more money. In my clients, I see associations made between freedom, security, and power. For Black Americans impacted by intergenerational racial, institutional, and class-based trauma, money worship feels like the progressive alternative to a money avoidant script. It says, I don't want to be the victim my ancestors were, and I'm going to buy my way out of it. It's the declaration that "cash rules everything around me" [C.R.E.A.M.].[2] It's the embracing of capitalism as a tool for salvation despite having no capital or control of the means of production. It's the belief that you can outwork centuries of systemic oppression and marginalization by using the very asset that was collateralized without the permission of your ancestors—your body. And, at the same time, it's not an entirely inaccurate belief, but it does serve to explain behavior, and that's what I'm here to do.

Money status is characterized by the notion that your self-worth equals your net worth. It's important to note that the difference between the money worship and money status scripts exists in the inward versus outward focus on money as a utility. The focus on accumulating money under the worship script theoretically makes you more capable and thus more powerful. Whereas the focus on accumulating money under the status script makes you appear more capable and is more about the outward demonstration of your wealth than actually having wealth. It's your classic "keeping up with the Joneses" scenario. Socially this script is reinforced from a young age where children are able to identify social status based on brand names and make hierarchical associations about themselves and others in relation to money. These associations often have an impact on their self-esteem or, as Dr. DeGruy calls it, vacant esteem.

---

[1] You can take the KMSI-R to find out your Money Script by visiting https://www.bradklontz.com/moneyscriptstest.
[2] This is from a song by Wu-Tang Clan.

Vacant esteem is described as the net result of three spheres of influence—society, community, and family. Similar to Bronfenbrenner's ecological systems theory, DeGruy examines the influences of institutional systems like laws, policies, and media, community systems or culture as I've referred to it in earlier chapters, and family systems. When these influences all promote a disparaging and limiting identity to which we believe we are confined, vacant esteem can be the result (DeGruy, 2005). While DeGruy makes it a point to emphasize that vacant esteem is a belief about one's worth and not a measure of their actual worth, the money status script creates a bridge between actual worth and self-worth. To me it explains the fixation on Nike Jordan sneakers throughout the 1990s and 2000s, iPhone versus Android debates during the 2020s, and the popularity of lifestyle marketing on social media where creators and influencers portray an onscreen lifestyle that is inconsistent with their actual lifestyle for clout.

When I think of money status, I think of two popular social media memes. There's one that poses the question would you rather have $100,000 or an 800 credit score and another that asks would you rather have dinner with Jay Z or $500,000. Both questions have polarizing responses that range from assessments of one's financial literacy to practical need for the money in either scenario. In both scenarios I believe the individual's response is going to be colored by the money script they most closely identify with. It's also important to note that you don't have just one money script and can demonstrate characteristics of multiple money scripts at the same time and that your money scripts can change over time. So it's not a fixed diagnosis but rather a means to define unconscious beliefs and behavior.

Money vigilance is characterized by vigilance or attentiveness to financial affairs. While typically considered to be positive, vigilance can lean on the extreme with excessive anxiety and distrust of others around money impacting your ability to enjoy the benefits and security that money provides

(Klontz et al., 2015). People with the money vigilance script tend to have higher incomes and net worths, could suffer from workaholism, and do not care for handouts, opting to work for their money.

I see money vigilance as a desire to operate within the financial system while still harboring mistrust of the system due to either a lived experience or inherited generational trauma. That mistrust is justified. It's the reason why willful nonparticipation in financial systems is often my counterargument when financial educators and policy makers declare that more financial literacy is needed in response to the unbanked or underbanked communities. Minorities, those with lower education levels, and those with lower incomes are more likely to be unbanked or underbanked (Liebowitz, 2018). I'll spend more time on the willful nonparticipation in financial systems in Chapter 10, but is it a surprise then that these groups influenced by financial trauma to the greatest degrees have found ways to operate outside of a traditional financial system? While the traditional framing of money vigilance centers on high-income earners with wealth to protect, I see similar patterns in individuals with limited means—those whose vigilance isn't about preserving assets, but surviving instability. Whether you're stockpiling cash in a brokerage or under a mattress, the emotional driver is the same: fear of loss and a desire for control.

Author Note: I've created additional resources to accompany this book including videos, micro courses, and more. Scan the following QR code or visit RahkimSabree.com/resources to access them.

Recognizing your money scripts and confronting the shame is a powerful act—but insight alone doesn't pay the bills or improve nonexistent financial behaviors. Healing starts with awareness but requires skill, specifically skill that can be learned and built upon. If financial trauma pulls you into survival mode, then financial education can serve as an anchor.

But not all financial literacy programming is created equal. Traditional approaches to financial education are often colonialized, are not trauma informed, and leverage guilt and shame-based approaches that often clash with individual values, goals, and past traumas.

In the next chapter, we'll explore how financial literacy can be used as an intervention strategy—not just for budgeting and credit, but for regulating your nervous system, reclaiming your autonomy, and rebuilding your financial identity on your terms. Not shame-based. Not one-size-fits-all.

Let's talk about what it *really* means to be financially literate . . . and financially well.

Chapter 9

Financial Literacy as an Intervention Method

When I sat down to write this book, I was determined not to write another financial literacy book. I wanted to focus on behavior and the emotional side of money. In many ways, I challenge the notion of financial literacy and its providers as leading with shame, guilt, and triggering financial trauma. My hope with this book is to help you redefine your relationship with money, removing guilt and shame and redefining success. So I'd be remiss if I spent time addressing the shortfall of financial literacy as a buzz phrase and its execution without providing perspective and a way forward for how this all fits into the idea of overcoming financial trauma and how to use financial education as an anchor rather than a magic bullet.

What was your introduction to financial literacy? Was it a course? A book? A social media influencer? Your parents? If you think back to that introduction, can you pinpoint the feelings or thoughts you held when introduced to the term financial literacy? My introduction to the business of financial literacy was the book *Rich Dad, Poor Dad*. The reason I specify the *business* of financial literacy is because when you examine the way financial literacy is packaged and presented, it seems almost offensive. It's mostly always marketed to you as some gatekept and hidden holy grail shrouded in phrases like "This is what the rich do" and "The secret to building generational wealth" or, my favorite, "This is how (insert name of ruling elite family) built their wealth!" The insult rests in the sleight of hand emotional manipulation that also ignores how centuries of wealth building rest on the exploitation of labor from people you may have genetic ties to—and resulting inherited trauma from.

You aren't taught "reading literacy" or "math literacy." You're simply taught how to read or apply mathematics, much in the same way you are taught about money. Even if you weren't taught to read or apply math, you would still learn how to talk and some manner of basic accounting through observation and by doing. It wouldn't be the Pythagorean theorem, but you would be able to recognize if Johnny had five apples and ate two that there are three left.

You begin learning about money emotionally first. What you see, what you hear, what you are told, and the lived experiences you have make up your money story. Different from money scripts, your money story or narrative is a consciously held belief based on your experiences with or around money. In the previous chapter I discuss a memory of experiencing money shame from the age of 7 and cite research that suggests we can make associations and develop habits at that age based on early experiences with money. Experiences not instruction. My parents did not sit me down and have conversations about how to use money beyond making sure I counted their change when I was sent to the store. I got my first paying job around the age of 15, at which point I'm sure I had made hundreds of cash transactions. Between the age of 15 and 18, I took money orders and cash over to property management to pay our rent, budgeted the monthly allotment of food stamps, held several part-time jobs, opened a bank account, and applied for college and student loans. Before I was introduced to the business of financial literacy, I was navigating financial decision-making relatively independently for a number of years. It was the business of financial literacy that made me feel like if I became financially literate that I would become rich. However, my intro to statistics course taught me a very important lesson: that correlation does not imply causation. Being financially educated is certainly a path to getting rich, but there are plenty of high-income people who have never taken a financial literacy course or workshop.

Financial Literacy as an Anchor

For the sake of clarity, I'm going to define and highlight the difference between financial knowledge and financial literacy as it was taught to me in the Association for Financial Counseling and Planning Education (AFCPE) curriculum. Financial knowledge is an awareness of facts or a transfer of information. Financial literacy includes financial knowledge plus the financial understanding of conceptual relationships and contextual factors that mediate and determine the financial outcomes for the individual (Durband et al., 2019). Using that definition, you gain financial knowledge through experiential learning, and that knowledge can be compounded with or without additional instruction to understand the relationships between individual financial variables (like what a credit card is, how to write a check, how to use a debit card) and the outcomes that result from engaging with those variables (like if I swipe this credit card to make a purchase, I will owe the creditor; if I write this check or swipe this debit card, the money comes from my account in a bank).

I have a money memory that illustrates the difference between having exposure to money but not literacy around it. As a child I would come home from school and see infomercials on TV always selling some gimmicky product that was supposed to make tasks easier. I mostly ignored them until the ones aimed at children came on. I don't remember what was being advertised, but I knew I wanted it, and I asked my mom. Immediately she told me no and that was the end of the discussion, but I was not one to give up so easily. I knew my mom had a checkbook and I'd seen her use it before, so one day while she wasn't home I waited for the commercial to come back on, and I grabbed her checkbook and went to write a check for the item. I quickly realized that not only did I not know how to write a check, but she had the checks with the carbon sheets behind them that copied what you wrote onto a receipt copy. Before I could figure out what was going on, I heard the keys rattling at the door, and I tossed my mom's checkbook under the sofa and forgot about it. It was never mentioned and I never brought it up, but I never tried to write a check from her checkbook again.

The child version of Rahkim recognized that the checkbook somehow paid for things but not how things were paid for (financial knowledge). I didn't realize I couldn't pull this off even if I was successful without my mom knowing because it would pull money from her bank account. I didn't understand the concept of check fraud (financial literacy). I didn't even know how I was going to mail out the check once it was written.

My financial literacy came when I started working in banking selling bank products and services to customers. I saw how these products worked in real time, how fees were triggered (and refunded), the impact of your credit score on lending decisions, and what happened when you spent money you didn't have in your bank account. I was frequently put in a position to solve a problem for a customer related to how they managed or mismanaged their money, and by osmosis I was able to apply these learnings to my own finances. Here's where the danger of the business of financial literacy shows up. Because I was aware of financial products and services and had regular access to individuals' account balances, their money stories, their occupations, etc., the scope of what was possible for me financially widened.

The Transtheoretical Model of Change (TTM) is a theoretical model developed by James O. Prochaska, Carlo DiClemente, and John C. Norcross that is broken down into five phases.

- Precontemplation
- Contemplation
- Preparation
- Action
- Maintenance

It's a model borrowed from mental health professions used in a financial setting via financial counseling. As an Accredited Financial Counselor® (AFC), we are taught that in the precontemplation stage, individuals have no intention to change, often resist acknowledging a problem exists, or may be unaware of the problem entirely (Durband et al., 2019).

Why does this matter? It matters because as I became more financially literate via my job, I also became more open to the idea of changing my circumstances by reading books, taking courses, attending seminars, etc. This made me a captive and targeted audience for people in the business of financial literacy making bold claims about what was possible for me to accomplish that was reinforced by what I saw on the job every day.

I want to be careful with my phrasing here because I'm not saying that everyone who monetizes financial education is a predator or bad actor. I know many people personally who are clear on their mission and who do not take advantage of people or over-promise and under-deliver on their services. What I do want to underscore here is that moving through this TTM based on what I was being exposed to combined with my money story and some sketchy sales tactics led me down a path to spending $12,000 on a program that was supposed to teach me how to become a real estate investor who could make back that money in as soon as 30 days. If I needed help funding the program—because you know, invest in yourself—I could ask family members to borrow money from their 401(k)s or lie to the credit card companies so I could get an increase in my credit line with the scripts they provided. At the time I was 23 years old with exactly $12,000 saved up that I intended on using as a downpayment on a house—the most I'd ever saved—and I handed it over because I was sold a dream under the guise of financial literacy.

I want to stay with this story for a moment because as I walk you through the actions I also want to walk you through the nervous system response occurring at that time. I was being worked on for three full days of this seminar that I paid $300 to attend. Over the course of three days I watched other people in the room be berated for "accepting mediocrity," "letting themselves and their families down," and "not having what it takes to build wealth." It was guilt and shame on steroids coming from these seemingly successful multimillionaire speakers. I was attending with a friend, and when we went home on night 2, I asked him, my girlfriend at the time, and my best friend if they thought I should do it. They all gave me the same answer, "If anyone can make this work, you can." I remember shivering violently as I laid in the bed that night not wanting to let my family or myself down but contemplating on spending all the money I had on something that was not guaranteed. At the end of day 3, when I decided to move forward, I remember shivering violently again; I couldn't breathe and I felt like I was going to throw up. All nervous system reactions. My body wanted to flee, and I was telling it to stay and fight. I wanted to be the one who changed the course of my family's financial future forever, and that had to start with me.

For years afterward, after I realized it was a money grab and that to be successful with the program I would need to pay more money for more mentoring, I didn't tell anyone about the experience. I didn't tell anyone I ever had the money, what I spent it on, or that it didn't work out how I expected it to. I was embarrassed, I was ashamed, and I felt isolated because of it.

No amount of studying or open mindedness can genuinely re-create the power of fear and uncertainty (Housel, 2020). In *The Psychology of Money*, Morgan Housel breaks down how your personal experiences with money are going to override your run-of-the-mill financial literacy curriculum every time, and not only that, but the decisions you do make are going to make sense to you based on your experiences in that moment. I can look back at that version of myself with what I know now and point out all the red flags and reasons why credible financial literacy was necessary in that instance. I was a banker and should have known better or googled reviews of the program beforehand. The problem was that the salespeople were aware of the reviews and openly discussed them in the seminar. We had finance professionals, real estate agents, lenders, marketers, nurses, and other professionals present as well. Housel shares an interesting stat in his book about lottery tickets. He shares that Americans spend more on lottery tickets than movies, video games, music, sporting events, and books combined and that the people who buy them mostly exist in the lowest income households in the United States. He then goes on to explain how crazy it is that the people in the lowest income groups account for most of the lottery spending but considers for a moment that the pain of their circumstances makes their spending seem worth it to them because what they're buying is not a lottery ticket; what they are buying is a dream . . . just like what I bought was a very expensive learning experience of a dream.

I'll bring this home by saying that clearly, as a financial services professional, I value a sound, credible, financial education as a cornerstone to holistic financial wellness. I believe financial education and the assumed application of that education sticks more when educational programming and instructors incorporate not just a systemic lens on why you might be navigating financial systems the way you do but also a lens on what is happening to your nervous system as you do so. To that end, financial education cannot be a solution; it can only serve as an anchor in getting to the solution. If the younger version of me was aware of how to check in with the alarms my body was giving off coupled with the financial knowledge and application of how to create and stick to a financial plan like buying a house, I wouldn't have been so susceptible to the seduction of the dream being sold to me. In hindsight, I do not regret having that experience. I believe in continuing education. I believe in the practice of investing in yourself. I'm proud of the version of me who not only believed in himself but surrounded himself with people who also believed in him. I would not be where I am today without him.

Financial Invincibility and High Income

Over the years I've come up against this narrative that people with high incomes are by default good stewards of money. Somewhere between the lines it perpetuates a dangerous normalization of workaholism in the sense that you begin to believe that if you make enough money, you don't have to be a good manager of money. This is especially true of people who come into large windfalls of money in a short period of time. A quick Google search will display varied statistics on lottery winners going bankrupt within five years; however, this wasn't a statistic I could find a credible source to point to. The fact remains, however, that entertainers, athletes, and lottery winners have demonstrated time and time again that without anchoring in the understanding of financial management they are quickly parted with their wealth.

I want to take this opportunity to introduce something I don't always see in conversations about wealth and money management, and that is an empathetic distribution of responsibility. I've spent much of this book decentering the individual as the problem and pointing back to the systems they navigate as the root cause. My job, however, is not to coddle or excuse personal responsibility but to highlight the realities of your experiences with money. In the previous example I discuss how rapidly the athletes, entertainers, and lottery winners are parted from their wealth, and certainly, there is the case to be made that financial education would slow that financial bleed. However, in reviewing the case studies of individuals who fit this criteria, or, even on a smaller scale, people who experience significantly higher levels of income than other members of their community, there is a social pressure and sense of obligation that surfaces where the individual might feel the need to—if it's within their means—buy everyone they love a house or a new car or jewelry. It could come from a place of generosity, a place of guilt, or external expectations. Traditional financial literary curriculums do not prepare you to establish financial boundaries or to come face-to-face with survivor remorse, the alienation from friends and family due to envy, the pressure to perform not just so that you can make a living but so that the people depending on you can continue depending on you. Financial literacy looks at how much money you start with (or make) and how much you end with and makes judgments about what happened in between. In March 2023 I wrote an article on Substack about NBA star Ja Morant due to the media spotlighting his behavior on social media (Sabree, 2023). In the article I introduce the phrase "money invincibility," which basically speaks to feelings of overconfidence due to the amount of money one has that results in them behaving as if their money will always be there. I used Morant as an archetypal example based on public opinion and the social commentary I saw on social media. So many people expressed concern that he was going to "mess up his opportunity" and get dropped because of his carrying on.

Money invincibility (which could also be described as overconfidence or extreme optimism) doesn't only show up in individuals commanding multimillion-dollar basketball salaries, record deals, or lottery winnings. That overconfidence shows up in the high earner as well. It shows up when you use mental or emotional budgeting instead of a spreadsheet or a numbers-based budget. It shows up when you dump all of your capital into a single stock, crypto coin, or business idea. It shows up when you overleverage credit cards for lifestyle expenses because you believe the job—thus the accompanying income—will be there next pay period so that you can catch up. And if you're a high earner operating from a place of scarcity, you might be afraid to splurge, but vigilance around money does not equate to literacy. I've made my case against financial literacy, and I've made a case for a credible financial education, so where does that leave you?

In the 3 E model of Overcoming Financial Trauma™, financial education falls into the second E for education shifting the focus from simply the demand for more financial literacy to a holistic, cultural, physiological, and trauma-informed approach that helps the education around money actually stick. If educators can teach people how to check in with themselves, with their bodies, then decisions can be made outside of the vacuum that screams emergency or threat.

Chapter 10

Banking and Financial Services

The banking industry was my professional home for a decade. I watched my dad work for a bank for a number of years in my childhood and later learned that my grandfather also worked in banking for a time. I guess you could say banking was in my blood. It's sort of a weird coincidence that we all ended up in banking professionally and that we all had a rather abrasive departure from the industry due to conflicts with our identity, or at least the version of us we wanted to be. Having been an insider, I learned how to navigate the banking system, its regulations, policies, compliance, and products with fluency, which served as the foundation of not only my financial education but my role as a financial educator. Banking is arguably the heart of the financial services industry, yet many are either unable or unwilling to engage in a banking relationship. In Chapter 5, I touched on some of the institutional trauma that exists within marginalized communities, some of which banks are historically—and present day—liable for. But this chapter is not about pointing the finger as much as it's about providing a mechanism for healing. When working with community banks and credit unions in a consulting capacity, one of the questions they all tend to be trying to answer is, how do we (re)gain the trust of prospective customers? It's a reasonable question to ask considering the second most cited reason for not having an account in 2023 was "Don't trust banks" according to a survey done by the FDIC.[1] That data tells a story of an avoidant trauma response as a symptom of a larger issue. It's also very telling that the first most cited response speaks to bank fees for their products specifically, that individuals surveyed "Don't have enough money to meet the minimum balance requirements."

Willful Nonparticipation Is Not Ignorance

I attended a community workshop on financial trauma that had representatives from several local banks and credit unions discussing the impact of financial trauma on customer relationships. What I loved about it was that it was rooted in sociology and historical context. What I didn't like about it so much was that it didn't actually acknowledge the trauma. Instead, it activated the nervous system responses of many of the participants who declared that they were mad; then they trauma bonded over the impact of their lived or observed financial traumas. Banking executives love data, and one of the data points this workshop offered was around the rates of the unbanked or underbanked broken down by ethnic group. There were also data points that highlighted net worth by ethnicity and the wealth gap between white families and Black families. The workshop got the audience hot and bothered and then offered financial education as the solution with a smooth transition into a sales pitch. I get it, we've all been there. I've made the same mistake. So I chimed in to offer a perspective both for the organizers and for the executives present: What if it's not about ignorance at all? What if they *do* understand the system—and reject it on purpose?

---

[1]FDIC, 2023. National Survey of Unbanked and Underbanked Households https://www.fdic.gov/household-survey/2023-fdic-national-survey-unbanked-and-underbanked-households-report

Or worse, what if they want to participate, but their history with banks or restrictive policies tells them it's not safe to? It was here that I developed and first used the phrase the **willful nonparticipation in financial systems**.

🔍 Concept Highlight: Willful Nonparticipation in Financial Systems

A refusal to engage in financial systems that have historically caused harm or represent a real or perceived threat to safety, autonomy, or dignity.

Banks are convenient. They know that, and they are constantly improving their offerings to become more so. With the advent of things like online and mobile banking, rates of adoption have resulted in a steady decline of in-person banking over the last decade with mobile banking as a primary method of account access seeing the greatest increase according to the FDIC. Despite the convenience of mobile banking, 5.6 million U.S. households remained unbanked in 2023. Rates among Black, Hispanic, and American Indian or Alaska Native households remain *several times* higher than white households. If this were just about convenience—or literacy—these numbers wouldn't persist. When viewed together, the data tells a different story: this is financial trauma. This is memory. This is avoidance as survival.

For many, nonparticipation isn't ignorance. It's a boundary.

So what can banks do to start establishing trust within these communities? They can own the hurt.

Own the Hurt—But Operationalize It

In 2005, JP Morgan Chase issued a public apology for its role in accepting for collateral and owning Black slaves via its subsidiaries between 1831 and 1865.[2] The public apology came complete with a five-year $5 million college scholarship for Black students in Louisiana and posted documents on ownership records online that are now no longer available. While now a relic of the past, this action by one of the largest banks in the United States demonstrates that banks are capable of acknowledging past hurts and actually doing something about it. While trauma is not something that anyone can just throw money at or apologize for with hopes it will go away, naming, acknowledging, and taking deliberate actions to heal that trauma can help metabolize it and create pathways for reconciliation. This can take a variety of forms that include a public acknowledgment on behalf of the industry even if the issuing bank can't or doesn't see its role in inflicting or perpetuating the trauma—because we're not just talking about slavery, we're talking about exploitative and predatory practices and capitalist norms, community listening sessions facilitated by trauma responsive practitioners, and annual transparency reports that include inclusive sales and lending practices, voice of the customer and complaint resolution, and data to bridge gaps in trust. Banks can also create or partner with community financial educators that provide bank-agnostic education on financial products/ services, provide leadership development on building financial empathy for executives, and reimagine sales language. Having worked in banking for a decade, I know that even the most ambitious of banks won't be able to operationalize this quickly, but that doesn't mean it shouldn't be attempted. In fact, it should not only be attempted once; there should be an ongoing commitment to implementing different aspects of this healing moving forward because as much as I hate to admit it, not only does this initiate community healing, but it'll make the bank more profitable in the long term. Still, individual healing within financial systems isn't just about banking institutions changing—it's also about how you, the consumer, make empowered choices from the inside out.

---

[2]The Guardian, (2005). Bank Admits It Owned Slaves https://www.theguardian.com/world/2005/jan/22/usa.davidteather

Financial Services for First Generation
Wealth Builders

If you're reading this book, chances are you have a bank account. If you don't, you likely use some money services business that allows you to make purchases and transfer funds electronically, and you know what that means—you have the power of choice. Financial service providers want your business. They want your business so badly, they're constantly tweaking their offerings to make *not using them* feel inconvenient. That is why they want your email and phone number, provide incentives for you to refer your friends, and make it easier for you to sign up than it is for you to leave. However, just because it's inconvenient for you to leave doesn't mean you shouldn't. It's important for you to recognize when your relationship with a financial service provider is causing you nervous system dysregulation and what you can do about it. I want to reiterate that your power is in your ability to choose, not how much money you keep with them, not how lucky they make you feel to be able to use their product over competitors via titles and rewards, and certainly not because they do the bare minimum with a highly recognizable name. For you to rebuild your trust with financial systems and institutions, they need to build trust with you, by earning it. This extends beyond banks and credit unions as well. Licensed financial professionals also need to earn your business and trust and not just by showing off their licenses or credentials. They need to show you—through their values, their treatment of you, and their curiosity—whether they genuinely care about where you've been and where you want to go. As someone in the financial services industry as an entrepreneur, this advice might feel counterintuitive. I've certainly had my seasons where any client felt like the right client, and any money felt like good money. The truth is if you are approaching money from a purely transactional perspective as either the client or the service provider, you are upholding the harmful nature of this system. If you are approaching money, however, from a healing perspective—which I believe is totally possible—then you are doing healing work, and you as either client or provider deserve to thrive in partnership.

The first time I worked with a financial advisor, it was because of a free perk associated with my employment. As an employee, we received a complimentary session with the advisor. I was excited about starting my investing journey, but I was a bit nervous. I had negative associations with the stock market but had a small savings I wanted to put to work. I scheduled an appointment that was rescheduled because a paying client walked in. No appointment, no notice, just deprioritized. When we finally got around to meeting, the advisor offered me a paid, managed plan that involved me dumping my money into some mutual fund family. When I declined the paid plan, I felt the advisor disengage with me and deprioritize me once again, handing me a packet with a list of fund families. There was no education, explanation, or inquiry into my goals, just a registering of no dollar signs and thus no business. That experience soured my perspective on licensed professionals so much that I made a personal declaration I would not get licensed to sell securities because I didn't want to make anyone feel the way that man made me feel. After growing up in the industry, I realize now that had that experience been better, I likely would have pursued the path of a Certified Financial Planner (CFP) way before I ever heard of the Accredited Financial Counselor (AFC). Had that experience been better, I likely would not be the one to write this book.

✎ Reflection Prompt

Think about the last financial service provider you engaged with.

Did you feel respected? Safe? Informed?

Did they ask questions—or just make assumptions?

When I wrote *Financially Irresponsible*, I wrote on the premise that it would be irresponsible for you to not at least be involved in your finances to the degree that you understand what's going on under the hood. I was a hardcore financial literacy enthusiast. I didn't have the lens on trauma I do now. To me, it was historical, perverse, and something I felt you could snap out of. While some of the thoughts I have on the topic have shifted, evolved, or changed altogether, I still maintain the original premise that you at least need to know what's going on at a high level. That involves establishing trust with the people you put in place to be on your money team. That involves asking questions and providing feedback. By going into these interactions and relationships with knowledge of your own money story and triggers to your fight-or-flight response, you can stop the infliction of financial trauma by either calling it out or taking your business elsewhere.

Understanding financial services is a situational awareness practice that shouldn't be confused with money vigilance (discussed in Chapter 8). Rather, it puts you in a position to best identify the financial service provider or institution that aligns with your goals and values. It also helps you to identify the extent to which your desires are realistic or possible. All financial institutions operate within a compliance and regulatory framework. Beneath that are operational guidelines that manage risk and customer satisfaction. These frameworks are in place to protect the institution and the consumer so that your next-door neighbor can't walk into your bank and access your bank account or financial information, as an example. A bank adhering to these guidelines is not inflicting financial trauma, even if the person trying to access information about the account is a relative trying to settle your estate if you pass away or acting as a power of attorney (POA) in the event of your incapacitation. I've seen many families navigate improperly structured or nonexistent estate plans and be left without access to their family members accounts. In these instances, because the bank cannot release funds to an unnamed party, it might feel like the bank is causing financial trauma by "stealing" your money. Because our brains cannot distinguish between a real or perceived threat, perception becomes reality, and the financial trauma you experience based on the perception the bank stole from you becomes a body response you pass on. This can be avoided by understanding financial services through education. Understanding financial services puts you in a position to distinguish between a real or perceived threat by grounding you in what actually is real and what steps you need to take to navigate those limitations. Estate planning, which includes having beneficiary designations, a will, and in some cases a trust, is a crucial element to understanding financial services if you intend on preserving and passing down any assets you accumulate throughout your life. It also serves to protect those family members or members of your community who are left behind to pick up the pieces. The reality is that your death, just like your birth, is going to cost somebody money. Educating yourself on the processes and limitations of your financial services provider is only half the battle. You will have to engage qualified professionals to create an estate plan.

Rebuilding Trust: What Comes Next for the System—and Everyone in It

Sometimes due to trauma you will project feelings or a response onto someone because they remind you of or represent the person who inflicted the original trauma. *Transference* refers to how a client's financial socialization (i.e., past financial-related experiences) and related emotions were not fully resolved (Durband et al., 2019, p. 69). While this reaction or response can show up in any area or relationship, it's important to be especially aware of how it shows up in working with financial professionals, and vice versa. In a process known as *counter transference*, the financial professional may subconsciously project their financial values and related advice onto you based on the experiences they've had individually or based on their experience with previous clients. This is a form of bias some financial professionals are educated in being aware of as we engage with clients around their own goals and values even if they differ from what we believe is best. As we've discussed in previous chapters, culture and financial socialization as well as financial trauma—including the mistrust of financial institutions and their professionals—will all be in the room with the professional and client. This is why trauma-informed and trauma responsive perspectives should also be present in the establishment of healthy interactions between client and professional and subsequently healthy behaviors in your relationship with money.

Q The Financial Professional's Mirror

If you're a financial professional—advisor, banker, counselor, planner, coach—this part is for you.

Before you prescribe, pitch, or plan, ask yourself:

- *Am I assuming this client lacks knowledge—or am I missing their lived experience?*
- *Am I listening to understand—or to position myself as the expert?*
- *Am I recommending what's best for them—or what's most familiar to me?*
- *Do I feel resistance or frustration when a client doesn't follow my advice? Why?*
- *Have I examined how my own money story influences my approach to theirs?*

This isn't about coddling or dumbing things down—it's about decentering your ego so you can actually *serve people.*

Transference goes both ways. If a client shows up guarded, defensive, or disengaged, it might not be about you.

But if that happens often?

Yeah. It might be.

Trauma-responsive finance starts with professional self-awareness. Not more credentials. Not another script. Start here.

I want to be clear here in saying that yes, I am pointing to the system and the harm it has caused, and yes, I am providing instruction for you to navigate within that very same system despite that harm. The reality is that there are few if any alternatives for you to navigate comfortably, especially if you earn a high income. By not being familiar with and working to heal inherent financial traumas related to navigating these systems while they are present, you open yourself up to greater possible exposure to trauma due to ignorance. You have to deal with taxes, complex financial planning, investment choices, and estate planning on top of how and what to spend on. You can't exist on autopilot because as I've mentioned previously, if you don't have a plan for your money someone else likely does and that plan is never to benefit you.

Even in instances where there is somewhat of a forced financial compliance, like your 401(k) or 403(b) company-sponsored retirement plans—forced in the sense that, if you don't participate now, you will regret it later—the company-sponsored financial wellness programs that explain them are usually boring, cookie cutter, and filled with jargon. That's if the company even has a financial wellness program in place and it's not just a rebrand-in-name of a recycled financial literacy program. You need a financial wellness program that drives less confusion, less shame, and more impact. (See Chapter 16 for how to build a trauma-responsive financial wellness program.) Yes, you should be aware of and take advantage of all the financial benefits associated with your compensation plan and you should advocate for clarity on the things you don't understand and more direct support if you don't have it, but it's not your fault that you don't understand. Many of these plans and benefits are still relatively new. The Roth IRA for example was born in 1998 (Housel, 2020). That's younger than I am (at the time of this writing). The 401(k) didn't exist until 1978. That's younger than both my parents.

If you are an HR professional reading this, this can explain low levels of engagement with your financial benefits. Not only are employees confused about what's available to them, but many are living paycheck to paycheck and don't feel confident about their financial well-being.

According to a 2024 Bankrate survey, 34% of workers are living paycheck to paycheck, including 24% of workers who earn $100,000 or more (Foster, 2024). A 2024 employee well-being survey from Bank of America also found that only 47% of workers rate their financial wellness as good or excellent, with 53% of respondents being men, 36% being women. It also demonstrates that only 39% of Black and 35% of Hispanic employees report high financial well-being compared to 58% of Asians and 50% of white employees (Bank of America, 2024).

The banking system wasn't built with everyone in mind—and for many, it became a source of trauma instead of trust. Even when taking into account Freedman's Saving & Trust, a bank Congress set up for newly emancipated Black Americans to help accelerate their economic empowerment (University of Chicago, 2020), there was the offloading of liabilities and mismanagement of depositors' funds that has contributed to "intergenerational mistrust of banks."

That's why I developed the TRUST™ Framework: a five-part approach to help unpack that damage and start rebuilding your financial identity in partnership with financial institutions on your own terms.

T is for Trauma-Responsive Approach, because healing starts with recognizing harm and taking action to reduce and heal that harm.

R is for Relationship Building, both with money and the institutions you engage with.

U stands for Unpacking Internalized Biases, the inherited beliefs that keep you stuck or that are projected onto you by financial professionals.

S is Supportive Frameworks—strategies that serve, not shame, like this TRUST Framework and the 3 Es framework I've structured this book under.

T is Training and Continuous Improvement, because growth isn't a one-time fix and it's not a fix that one person or one organization can institute on their own. Training is essential. This isn't about making peace with the system—it's about reclaiming your power within it.

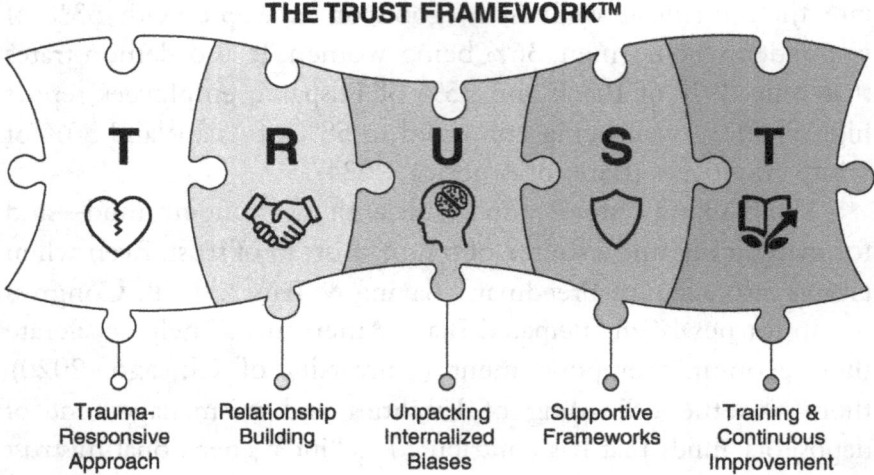

THE TRUST FRAMEWORK™

| Trauma-Responsive Approach | Relationship Building | Unpacking Internalized Biases | Supportive Frameworks | Training & Continuous Improvement |

Chapter 11

Budgeting, Saving, and Financial Planning with a Healing Mindset

One of the earliest money lessons I learned was that I should save money. I didn't learn what I should be saving for or why I should save, just that I should save money. I was taught to save in reaction to something. I didn't know it then, but the emphasis the adults in my life placed on saving came from the burden of them not having much if anything saved themselves. The issue with reactionary saving is that there's always something that comes up causing you to dip into that savings, creating a saving loop that involves an accumulation phase where you are saving for a particular goal; the summit phase where you reach that goal (or you don't because something derailed it); and a distribution phase where you deplete your savings, you start at 0, and engage in the saving loop again and again.

The cyclical nature of this activity can be seen in diet and fitness fads as well. You rush into the gym in January and February to work off all the holiday sweets and junk food, you lose a few pounds and start getting your summer body together, and then fall and winter come and—if fitness is not a lifestyle for you—you fall off, doomed to repeat the cycle in January. What if you made saving a lifestyle like some people do with fitness? Reactionary saving, just like a reactionary diet and exercise, keeps you on a hamster wheel of pseudo progress as you take two steps forward just to take three steps back. This kind of save-spend-repeat cycle mirrors trauma loops—brief control followed by collapse, which only reinforces the shame.

When I hear of financial educators discussing saving, it's almost always accompanied by a lesson on why you need a budget. But the word *budget* tends to cause a mental and physical reaction in the people I discuss it with. Most people who come to me experiencing some sort of financial chaos admit to either not having a budget or doing mental accounting rather than a formal budgeting process because "they know what's coming in and what's going out." In this chapter, we're going to discuss the reason why your budget fails you, the exercise of saving versus intentional saving practices, and financial planning with a healing mindset.

The Problem with Traditional Budgets

Personally, I'm a big fan of the traditionally recommended budgeting structures. I recommend the pay yourself first method where you take a percentage of what you make before paying any bills or expenses and put it into long-term savings or investments. I've seen others have success with the 50/30/20 rule where 50% of your after-tax income goes to needs, 30% goes to wants, and 20% goes to saving, and the zero-based budget where all of your after-tax income is planned for each pay period so that $0 is left over.

I believe that it's important to have a plan for your money and to make sure you are adhering to that plan. Budgeting allows you to do both by recording your planned income, actual income, and expenses over a period of time. I also believe that budgeting is tossed around as an easy solution to people's spending problems, inability to save, and excessive consumption. In this way, the concept of a budget can feel like a punishment to a trauma-impacted brain. Furthermore, the articulation of budgeting as simply a means to track your spending does nothing for the individual who is aware of their spending but doesn't feel they have the ability to stop. Budgeting can work on its own in theory, with buy-in from the individual needing the budget. However, trauma-responsive budgeting is more effective, especially in response to a dysregulated nervous system.

Why do you need a trauma-informed or responsive approach to budgeting? Because budget failures are often a result of capitalism and advertising strategy discussed in Chapters 3 and 5, which includes a culture of consumerism and social engineering that uses advertising to connect feelings with the products being sold. You develop a chemical need to buy the things you see pushed in front of you via dopamine as a way to escape the dysregulation you are experiencing and shamed for not being disciplined enough. Budgeting is offered then, again feeling like a punishment, to keep you in line and, regardless of income level, is context blind and classist.

Imagine sitting in a room full of people wanting to regain control of their financial situations because they live paycheck to paycheck and hearing the instructor say, "Well, you just need to do a better job budgeting." You look over the numbers, and you haven't taken a vacation in years. Your discretionary income is relatively nonexistent, and you're struggling to cover even basic living expenses. Bravely, you push forward and share these details to which the response is "Well, maybe you just need to make more money!"

While it is true that you can eliminate only so many expenses before you need to increase your income, it's also a reflection of the system that you can't afford basic expenses on your current income alone. That's not a personal failure or a budgeting failure, it's a systemic one. If this scenario was applied to a high-income earner who simply has too many discretionary expenses, then a budget might help. There is a difference between having too many discretionary expenses and not having enough income. That difference exists in an often undiscussed financial classism that surfaces from financial educators, particularly those speaking to mixed crowds. Although the concept of budgeting itself may come with triggers, strategically and empathetically placed, it will land well if positioned as a tool for liberation rather than punishment. If it's positioned as a practice that simply lets you know exactly where you are and gives you the opportunity to decide where you would like to go without guilt or shame, just choices. Those choices are going to be influenced by a variety of factors, the most basic of which come down to safety.

Saving as Safety Not Sacrifice

Most people start to save because they have to. Either they were cautioned in childhood like I was, or they learned the hard way that in a world where it costs money to be born and to die, you need to have something put away somewhere. Even the most financially secure people still need to save to maintain that security. The difference is, their savings tend to look more sophisticated—often in the form of assets that hold value, grow, or produce income. This is often the rationale behind investing. You put money into something with the expectation that thing will do one of the three things I mentioned. Of course, you also take on the risk of fluctuations in value, but people generally do not invest with the intention of seeing the value go to zero. Generally, when people invest, they are making decisions today that they expect will benefit them in the future, so it can be assumed that when people do not invest they either (A) haven't thought that far ahead, (B) don't expect to get there, or (C) have no idea what they need to do to get there.

In the case of person A, they may be entertaining the dangerous illusion that they have time or default to the idea that they have time and will later get to it because it doesn't feel like there is enough time today. This person is overwhelmed with tasks, expectations, and obligations. They may have little bandwidth to entertain anything outside of their routine, and every day is today. What's interesting about person A is that they can be a high-income workaholic or someone low-income navigating a poverty cycle.

In the case of person B, they almost certainly have trauma in the sense that they embrace a YOLO (you only live once) mentality. They may feel that the money they earn should be enjoyed at the moment because life could end at any time, so why waste it saving? They believe that if they make it to the future they will deal with it when they get there—no plan just vibes.

Person C may have the income and flexibility to save financially but has no idea what to do with the money. Do they put it into bonds, a CD, stocks, real estate, or crypto? This person has a willingness to save but, because they don't know what to do, experiences analysis paralysis and opts to do nothing—a freeze response. This isn't laziness. It's self-protection.

Financial Planning

Financial planning serves as a needed resource for the various life transitions that undoubtedly have financial implications. Yet, when discussing financial planning with the average person there are often two assumptions made that carry some truth. The first is that it's expensive and a high barrier to entry, which for some planners—especially those who charge based on assets under management or aum—can be true for even a high-income low net worth client. The second is that financial planners are synonymous with retirement planning, or that's their primary focus. Of course, financial planners look at all stages in the life cycle of their clients that can extend to their spouse, parents, and children. Many people don't seem to know the intricacies of a financial planner and their roles and responsibilities. While I won't spend this book's precious real estate breaking down the nuances of financial planning, I do want to focus in on retirement and estate planning as functions of the financial planning professional.

Question: How do you prepare someone who hasn't inherited assets or instructions to leave assets and instructions to those they will eventually leave behind?

Question: How do you prepare someone who doesn't believe they will live long enough to retire or that they won't be able to afford to retire to engage in retirement planning and implementation?

Both of these questions can be asked through a lens of education and financial trauma with the latter being a bit more complex to navigate and deal with. If you are someone who hasn't met with a financial planner, even just for a consultation, I implore you to do so. Many financial planners will charge a flat rate for a one-time plan but can offer a variety of services including subscription models, commission models (on products they sell you), and some even offer pro bono planning. If you find or suspect that financial trauma influences your ability or willingness to engage in the financial planning process, you may want to seek out a financial planning professional with education in financial therapy or seek out a financial therapist.

While budgeting, saving, and financial planning alone may not be new topics in and of themselves to you, the purpose of this chapter is to change the lens by which you approach these behaviors. Are you budgeting, saving, and planning because you feel it's what you should be doing despite feelings of discomfort? Or are you approaching these behaviors from a place of wholeness, safety, security, and comfort? Micro behaviors in each category like expense tracking, creating a freedom fund, or initiating a financial planning conversation just to see what is possible can help to regulate a trauma-impacted nervous system, avoid additional misinformation-based financial trauma, and encourage a greater affinity toward taking action.

Part III

EXECUTION: IMPLEMENTING STRATEGIES FOR FINANCIAL HEALING

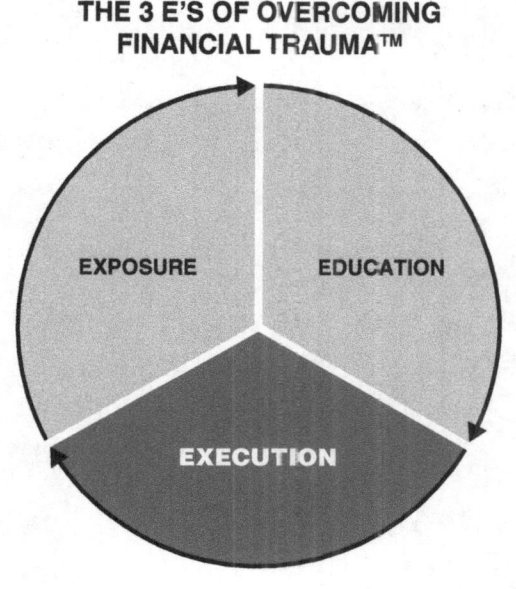

THE 3 E'S OF OVERCOMING FINANCIAL TRAUMA™

Part II

EXECUTION:
IMPLEMENTING
STRATEGIES
FOR FINANCIAL TRADING

Chapter 12

Rewriting Your Financial Narrative

S o far we've spent time understanding your money script (the subconscious beliefs you developed in childhood) and your money story (the culmination of lived financial experiences that helps you make sense of your past money decisions). Both your unconscious money script and your conscious money story can be influenced by financial trauma but they weren't created exclusively within the spectrum of trauma, and therefore financial trauma doesn't have to define your financial narrative of the future.

Your financial narrative was shaped by the programming you absorbed: lessons passed down by parents, community, cultural values, religious teachings, and media. Your financial narrative may have been crafted to protect you or it is simply reflections of the world based on that programming. Simply put, your money narrative is a belief system you have about money made up of your money scripts, your money stories, and external influences on your beliefs about money.

Term	What It Is	How It Shows Up
Money Script	A subconscious belief about money that is often formed in childhood and passed down generationally	"Money is the root of all evil." "Rich people are greedy." "More money will solve all my problems."
Money Story	A personal experience or memory that shaped how you relate to money	"When I was 10, I saw my parents fighting about money. Now I avoid talking about money."
Financial Narrative	Your overall belief system about money, combining money stories, money scripts, and outside influence	"I have to hustle nonstop because my safety only comes from financial control."

Financial trauma often magnifies the most painful parts of your financial experiences, which become part of your financial narrative, whether that's experienced in the workplace, through the financial systems and institutions you navigate, via painful experiences that have been passed down through your genes, and even what you've observed other people with money doing. It etches certain beliefs deeper, makes others feel non-negotiable, and sometimes freezes your financial behavior in ways that no longer serve you.

For example, my financial narrative had largely remained unchanged despite achieving levels of financial success beyond what I believed was possible at one time. When experiencing a bit of financial instability as an entrepreneur, my financial narrative began to surface. It took a financial therapy session with another financial therapist for me to realize that I had largely viewed myself as a money manager and not a generator of money. This is partly because before I could generate income on my own, I played an integral part in helping to *manage* the money in my mom's household. When I would grow to make my own income in a traditional nine-to-five environment, I continued with my previous narrative—I am a good manager of money— and built on it with education of financial products and services. As an adult, I never had to develop a hustling mindset to make money because my needs were largely taken care of by the security of my paycheck. While this narrative served me as an employee, it caused deep frustration as an entrepreneur because you can't manage money you do not have. You need to generate it. This speaks again to the belief that financial literacy is the magic bullet to solve all financial woes. Sometimes the decisions made by people who would be viewed as financially illiterate are decisions made due to a lack of money, not information carved deeper by their own money narratives.

Maybe you have a story too—one that served you for a time, but no longer fits who you are becoming.

To rewrite your financial narrative, you have to first have an understanding of the existing one and how it may be influenced by financial trauma. It doesn't involve pretending your early programming never happened or that you simply outgrew it because your financial station improved. It's about consciously choosing what stays, what evolves, and what needs to be left behind or repositioned. It's about moving from automatic reaction to intentionality. For me, the "money manager" narrative can still serve me when necessary, but it doesn't have to define me or my behavior exclusively.

As we move into the execution phase of the 3E™ Framework, this chapter is your invitation to stop letting an outdated narrative dictate your future—and start writing one that reflects the person you're becoming.

Claiming Your Financial Identity

When you've spent most of your life being reactionary around money—especially when it comes to familial expectations, generational beliefs you may have inherited, economic hardship, or just the hustle that comes with playing the capitalism game—it can be easy to forget or believe that you have any say at all in your financial narrative. This isn't one of those "you've got to pull yourself up by your bootstraps" conversations, but I am going to point to the role of personal awareness and personal responsibility in your being both on the offensive and defensive when it comes to your financial health and navigating financial trauma. Rewriting your financial narrative starts here: by consciously claiming the financial identity you want to step into, instead of staying chained to the one you've been operating on autopilot.

Financial healing isn't just about fixing or even diagnosing problems. In many ways, it's about practicing a new or enhanced identity around money. The things you think about, tell yourself, and the behaviors you exhibit become reflections of that identity.

Ask yourself, who am I becoming financially? And you align your choices, habits, and mindset to that answer—an answer that you control. That you are in charge of.

You don't need to become a millionaire or earn a six-figure salary to write a new financial narrative. You don't need an 800+ credit score or a maxed-out 401(k). You need to make a decision—a deliberate, values-driven decision about how you will move through your financial life from this point onward. You can pull from all of your past learnings, the tools you've used in survival, and the reactions to previous trauma, to capitalism, to toxic workplaces, to entrepreneurship, etc., and you create a version of that narrative that is not reactionary but intentional. Sometimes, you may need to remind yourself of this new narrative. You will want to revert to a familiar chaos, and the earlier parts of this book have explained why. Your narrative should remind you of your safety and that you today are not the person you were yesterday or a year ago or when you were a child. You today get to draw a line in the sand and make decisions for you of tomorrow.

Replacing Old Financial Narratives

Rewriting your financial narrative isn't just about repeating a new affirmation until you believe it. Although affirmations can certainly be part of it, real change—the kind that sticks—happens when you integrate new narratives across your mind, your emotions, and your body. This work is supported by multiple disciplines, from financial therapy to trauma science to neuroplasticity research. Healing trauma involves recognizing, accepting, and moving through pain—**clean pain**.[1] It often means facing what you don't want to face . . . the alternative paths of avoidance, blame, and denial are paired with dirty pain.

The mistake I see many people make (myself included) when trying to incorporate narrative change both financially and otherwise is that they believe if they think really, really hard, they can *will* their way into healing. Dr. Joe Dispenza's work in *Becoming Supernatural* highlights something critical, though: as long as you are anchored emotionally, mentally, and traumatically to the past, you can't create a new future. You can know the

---

[1] Clean pain and dirty pain are concepts introduced in the book *My Grandmother's Hands* by Resmaa Menakem that describe healthy and unhealthy ways to grow through or avoid trauma.

financial fundamentals; the products, the services, how and what to invest in, etc., but if your body is locked into fear, scarcity, shame, or survival states, you will unconsciously and involuntarily re-create what you're trying to leave behind. Some of this healing work you will find in the pages to come sound like alchemy. You are transmuting one form of energy (financial trauma) into another on a mind level, a body level, and even a soul level. Let's break down the three with solid examples you can start practicing right now, today.

Key Points:
- Your financial narrative isn't rewritten in one big move—it's practiced through small, consistent choices.
- Micro-habits are the bridge between old survival-based reactions and new intentional behavior.

Mind Level

Checking bank accounts once per week without judgment and documenting spending, saving, and debt elimination in comparison to the values and goals you are adopting for the future.

Scheduling a "money date" with yourself where you go deep on financial behavior over the previous 30 days with projections for the next 30 days once per month. Ask yourself if your actions are consistent with the version of you that you are trying to be or the version of you that you are trying to leave.

Body Level

Practice breath work to both clear your mind and bring you back to the present moment when you are feeling anxious about money.

Perform body scans of where you feel it in your body when your financial boundaries are crossed, when you are tempted to engage in retail therapy, or when you fight about money. Notate what you feel, where you feel it, and what triggered this body response.

Soul Level

Practice future-self visualizations by imagining the version of you five years from now fully immersed in your new financial narrative. Identify behaviors and beliefs you have that you won't carry forward and what that does for you. Do you allow yourself to make more money without guilt? Are you charitable? Are you reactionary or intentional?

Reflect on your ancestors who have passed on their traumas through DNA. Let them know that because of their sacrifices and strength you are here. Reflect on the survival skills they had to develop around money and resources and assess whether they serve you today. Journal your gratitude to them for their gifts and how you intend to honor them by clearing old patterns and creating new ones.

By replacing old patterns, habits, and beliefs with new ones, you are no longer simply wishing for change but actually creating change, and you're doing so consistent with the way your brain works. What I mean by this is you're actively working to create new neural pathways by replacing old patterns that exist on autopilot with behaviors that are aligned with a new version of yourself that you chose, curated to experience safety, which is what your brain is wired to do. In my work with clients, one of my primary goals is to help them first recognize their safety in the moment, within their circumstances, and within their life.

Financial therapists often start with identifying money scripts through the use of tools like the KMSI-R.[2] This and narrative therapy models help the financial therapist and their client to name, challenge, and create distance between the individual and the old narrative. While this may be an effective starting point among my peers, I believe that the context by which the traditional lens on financial therapy broadly—and financial trauma specifically—

---

[2] Klontz Money Script Inventory-Revised, developed in 2014, has been used as a streamlined alternative to the KMSI for use in research and with clients.

doesn't account for all of the variables introduced in this book. That trauma, even if tied to our finances, demands more than narrative or cognitive behavioral frameworks to work through and metabolize. I will discuss financial therapy and alternative forms of healing in Chapter 15, but for now I believe these exercises are effective in helping to rewrite your financial narrative, but not the finish line in overcoming financial trauma.

Exercise Rewiring Thought Patterns:[3]

Write down one to three money beliefs you know are no longer serving you.

For each one, answer:

- Where did this belief come from?
- Is it 100% true?
- What belief would I rather embody instead?

When you name a belief instead of operating blindly under it, you weaken its hold and can start to choose differently.

It's important to note that the answers you come to as a result of doing this exercise are going to depend largely on your existing financial narratives. If you believe that you are a bad person because you are carrying debt, then your answer is going to be reflective of that. If you believe that you have to struggle or be a workaholic, your answer is going to be reflective of that. That is why the prior sections of this book around exposure and education exist and come before these exercises. The goal is to offer you another perspective on your relationship with money that doesn't depend on guilt or shame while simultaneously offering you a path for personal accountability and increased financial health. Take your time with these exercises. Do them again and again. Some breakthroughs will happen on your own. Others may require you to work with a financial therapist or another trauma-informed financial professional as an unbiased observer to get to that breakthrough.

---

[3] This exercise is inspired by *Facilitating Financial Health* by Klontz, Kahler, & Klontz.

Exercise Engaging the Body[4]

The reactions you have around money that contribute to financial stress, financial anxiety, vicarious or experienced financial trauma, etc., don't just create stories that become your financial narratives—they're stored in your body via your nervous system. When you've experienced rejection, loss, faced scarcity, had a boundary crossed, witnessed or experienced financial abuse, or were made to feel shame related to money, your body remembers.

Whether it's tension in your shoulders related to financial stress, tightness in your chest or stomach related to financial anxiety, your heart rate increasing in anticipation of a fight or flee response, these physical reactions are stored as memories long after the perceived threat is gone. These somatic memories outlast the initial trauma by years and can even be passed down to your children and your children's children.

The next time you engage with a money or money adjacent experience (looking for a job, checking your account to make sure you have enough money, making a big purchase, etc.):

- Pay attention to your body.
- Where do you feel tension, constriction, heat, or numbness? What is being activated for you?
- Breathe into it. Acknowledge it. Recognize that you aren't broken; your body is remembering.

Building awareness of somatic memory allows you to rewrite your felt experience with money in addition to your thoughts and narratives.

As you build awareness of how your body holds on to financial memory, you create space to give it something new to hold. The next step is embodiment—teaching your nervous system what safety and success feel like through daily intentional practice.

---

[4] This exercise is inspired by the book *The Body Keeps the Score* by Van Der Kolk.

Exercise Embodying a New Financial Self[5]

Visualization, elevated emotional states (like gratitude, empowerment, and peace), and intentional daily actions or routines are tools you can use to teach your body what safety and abundance feel like right now. When you hear about mantras and affirmations, these are ancient practices that still work to this day, if they are done correctly. You cannot wish your way into healing or wealth. You have to embody it as if it is here now.

Spend two minutes each day imagining yourself successfully embodying your new financial self.

Feel the gratitude as if it's already real.

Picture yourself engaging with financial systems calmly, confidently, and joyfully.

Let your nervous system rehearse what success feels like. Just as the brain cannot distinguish between a real or perceived threat, it will not distinguish between your real and perceived safety. Choose peace. Choose safety.

These three layers, mind, body, and soul, don't function in silos as we're often taught to view money. They're a unified action to heal the internal body systems that trauma rewires. You've now got tools to disrupt old beliefs, release stored fear, and reprogram how you show up with money. You're literally rehearsing a new reality.

As you practice these exercises, I want to remind you that rewriting your financial narrative isn't just a mental decision, just as the trauma we experience isn't just a mind event. They are both full-body, full-belief system rewrites. It's okay if you feel pulled into old habits and patterns. Recognize that even in the midst of the chaos it may bring, it is what is familiar to your brain, and familiarity equals safe. Teach your mind and your body how to embrace true safety by practicing and modeling safety. If you have

---

[5] This exercise is inspired by the book *Becoming Supernatural* by Dispenza.

trouble doing this alone, there is help available through profession-als and through community.

Be kind to yourself. You will not undo all of your years of pro-gramming and inherited trauma in one session.

One small choice, one new story, one new experience at a time.

Rewriting your financial narrative is not a one-time event—it's a daily practice of choosing who you want to be with money, even when your nervous system wants to run the old script. When I learned about my money manager narrative and realized I could *choose* to adopt one of a money generator, I felt encouraged, but it didn't immediately stick. I have to actively remind myself of what has served me in the past and what I need to serve me in my present and future. This intentionality is the first real act of reclaim-ing financial autonomy by acknowledging the influences that have led you to where you currently are—without guilt or shame and choosing to move forward anyway. Financial trauma as I've defined it throughout this book is a pervasive psychological, emotional, and physiological response to so many variables you are socialized to believe and accept as normal. Whether personal, systemic, inher-ited, or observed, your brain and body don't care about the source of the harm or threat; they simply respond to it. Rewriting your narrative is the first tool I offer you in interrupting that response. The tools in the chapters to come will also help to empower you to take action and become a victor rather than a victim. Choose your narrative. Choose yourself. And if you forget tomorrow, choose again.

Chapter 13

Setting Financial Boundaries

In the journey toward financial healing, it's important to set and maintain boundaries with your time, energy, and finances. In Chapter 6 I discussed how the expectations of family, society, and religion may influence financial trauma, especially in high-performing first-generation wealth builders, but sometimes the person you most need to set financial boundaries with is yourself. Financial boundaries are the limits you set to protect your financial well-being; they ensure your resources align with your values and goals. This chapter will discuss the intricacies of financial boundaries and explore why you may struggle with them, how to establish them, and how to enforce them effectively.

Understanding Financial Boundaries

What Are Financial Boundaries?

Financial boundaries are personal guidelines you can establish to manage your financial interactions with yourself and others. These boundaries dictate how you spend, save, lend, and discuss money, ensuring that your financial decisions reflect your values and priorities. The reason I emphasize having boundaries for yourself in this chapter is that unlike most discussions on financial boundary setting where you are acting in opposition to an individual's outward influence on your decision-making, viewing boundaries from a trauma-responsive perspective demands that you be conscious and aware of how your responses to trauma may bend or break your established boundaries, impacting the systems you set up, like your budget, triggering a guilt/shame cycle, or convincing yourself that it's okay because "you deserve it."

Several factors contribute to the difficulties I've seen in clients' setting and maintaining financial boundaries, including:

- Cultural influences
- Familial patterns
- Trauma and attachment styles
- Nervous system regulation

Cultural Influences

In Chapter 6 I discussed how our view of culture needs to be expanded to accommodate things like workplace culture, consumerism culture, regional culture, religious culture, etc. Cultural norms often dictate and justify financial behavior that may contradict your financial goals. These norms can include an expectation to support others financially or even taboos around discussing money. The culture of individualism necessitates that everyone has their own— their own car, own house, own bank account, etc. While private ownership is not a problem in and of itself, it rapidly increases the rate of consumption and the up-front demand to support individual needs. In a four-person household, there may be three or four vehicles, one for each person of driving age and ability. That's four different car payments with insurance and gasoline demands. This has a great impact on personal economic systems that boil up to familial economic systems that boil up to regional systems, on up.

Familial Patterns

In addition to the broader cultural influences, there may be specific familial dynamics that blur the lines between individual and collective financial responsibilities. Financial therapy recognizes a money disorder called *financial enmeshment* or a phenomenon when parents use money to manipulate a child to satisfy an adult need (Klontz et al., 2015, p. 56). Although the majority of money disorders have not yet been identified by the mental health community (Klontz et al., 2015, p. 36), there are diagnostic criteria for this and other money disorders used by financial therapists and some financial planners. The research by Klontz et al. on financial enmeshment highlights how the overly intertwining nature of family members' financial lives—particularly that of parent and child—can lead to blurred boundaries and financial dysfunction. However, this lens on familial financial behavior may be a reflection of individualist values stemming from capitalism and may act in direct opposition to indigenous and communal family norms. These disorders can also surface as a reaction to systems of oppression that force families to lean more heavily on each other financially or push family members out into the world prematurely. For example, in families relying on public assistance, an 18-year-old's job doesn't just represent independence—it threatens the family's housing stability. Section 8 regulations count that income toward household totals (HUD.gov), which can raise rent or disqualify the entire family. Thus, the idea that once a child turns 18 they need to move out or contribute to the household becomes a painful survival reaction that may create feelings of animosity, unhealthy or nonexistent boundaries, and distorted expectations. The unprepared 18-year-old who leaves may then seek out assistance on their own to survive based on need and familiarity to what they have seen their parents do, creating a vicious cycle of systemic dependence and abuse.

Trauma and Attachment Styles

Attachment styles and trauma responses can influence financial behaviors as you learn to associate money with access, power, love, or influence. The term *financial fawning*, coined by Chantel Chapman, founder of The Trauma of Money, refers to using money as a tool to seek security and attachment, often through people-pleasing behaviors. As pointed out in Chapter 7, fawning is a trauma response that can surface when you can't fight, flee, or freeze your way out of perceived or real danger. Financial fawning can look like avoidant behaviors to avoid confrontation or can look like lavish and excessive gift giving resulting from overspending to gain favor or approval. Think about the last round of drinks you purchased or when you picked up the tab for a group. Think about how you communicate love or affection through gift giving. You may feel as though your love language is acts of servitude when really you are demonstrating a trauma response! Attachment theory, developed by attachment researcher John Bowlby, is a popular mental health framework used by financial therapists in dealing with couples. But your attachment style may influence more than how you relate to your romantic partner, extending into how you relate to friends, authority figures, and other family members.

Nervous System Regulation

You may have great command of the word "no" in enforcing your financial boundaries with others but make frequent exceptions to the boundaries you set for yourself financially. Similar to the idea of a cheat meal when adhering to a strict diet, you may find ways to justify overspending or splurging outside of your defined budget. While planned rewards are generally recommended to avoid burnout and a loss of motivation, retail therapy, as it's popularly referred to, exemplifies this behavior as a way to relieve stress or tension due to the resulting dopamine response. This behavior can compound as it's not a purely financial event. With money providing access to things such as drugs, alcohol, gambling, or everyday items, the nervous system response can turn into money disorders like compulsive buying disorder, gambling disorder, hoarding disorder, financial denial, and financial infidelity.

The Three-Part Financial Boundary Setting Framework

In my workshops on financial boundary setting, I've developed a framework for how to establish and maintain healthy financial boundaries as dictated and defined by you. I believe this approach is necessary due to the varied nature of possible audience values, goals, and circumstances influencing the erection of boundaries.

The three-part framework includes the following.

Audit Your Values

It's important to start by auditing your individual values. What is the role of culture, relationships, career, etc., on your financial goals and behavior? Where are your financial boundaries in these areas weak or nonexistent? What is driving you to want to achieve different things financially? Sometimes the financial anxiety or stress you feel will come from anticipated expectations or unspoken burdens you pick up because they were modeled for you in your early socialization with money through observation or direct experience. You are empowered to list, define, maintain, or eliminate the things that no longer serve you from a values perspective. You are empowered to adopt new ones and to change the culture that influences those values.

Establish SMART Goals

SMART goals are more than just things you'd like to have happen. They are intentional and planned out with measurable and attainable milestones along the way. There is a difference between saying I want to save more and saying I will put $25 a paycheck into a specific savings account for a specific goal. One of the questions I often ask my clients when they articulate their goals to me is, is that goal something you want to achieve or something you believe you're supposed to achieve? Sometimes the goals I see my clients set for themselves come from a financial influencer or advice from someone else that sounds good. While great for a frame of reference, the problem with adopted goals like these is that they are not value aligned to what the individual actually wants to do, which will create resistance and cause frustration when the goal is not achieved or even attempted. When establishing boundaries, it's important to tie those boundaries to a goal for yourself that is rooted in your safety. Safety for you doesn't have to look like a threat of imminent harm; it can look like having enough money to cover an unexpected bill, putting money aside for retirement, or increasing your net worth as a hedge against inflation. If safety is at the center of your decision-making, you can develop a bias toward taking action that ensures that safety that includes upholding the boundaries you set for yourself and others.

Communicate

It's important to practice communication strategies, verbiage, and providing alternatives that align with your values. Sometimes you may conflate your desire to spend time with someone as a money event when you can achieve the same goal without spending money at all. That's why the first part of this framework focuses on identifying your values. Your values may be very aligned with spending time with friends and family, for example, that may make it difficult to establish a financial boundary with them if you or they feel the only way to do that is to go to a bar or restaurant or travel. When you are able to separate your values from the act of spending money, you can confidently communicate that while you'd love to spend time with them, it's not in your budget to do so in a way that involves money. You can then follow up with an alternative way to accomplish that goal, like inviting them to go for a walk or to visit each other's homes. I had a client who loved to entertain and, despite curating a warm and welcoming environment in their home, found themselves constantly going out for drinks with friends despite drowning in debt. When I suggested that they could decline the drink invite in a way that didn't sound like a flat out no and instead invite their friends to their home, a light bulb went off for them as they recognized they could adhere to their values without experiencing the shame of sharing their financial situation or creating an environment where, if they chose to, they could share while not putting pressure on their friend group to cover their expenses.

Finally, it's important to emphasize here that "no" is a complete sentence. If something exists outside of the boundaries you set for yourself financially, you are not obligated to elaborate or explain why.

Survivor's Remorse and Financial Boundaries

Survivor's remorse is often a recognized but understated feeling I see in the clients I work with. Many times it's shrouded in shame and guilt perceived as part of the burden that comes with financial success. There's a quiet grief that settles in when you realize that your wins have created distance not only between an old version of yourself but associated connections—friends, family, community. Isolation can be a byproduct of the individualistic values associated with capitalism, and the guilt you feel isn't irrational; it's relational. Your success becomes a mirror that reflects to others, not what you've overcome to get there but what they don't have access to. How many times have you experienced an awkward silence when you mention a promotion? A new accomplishment? A new purchase? The sting of resentment in the "must be nice" texts or the unspoken expectations that you will pick up the bill, fix the problem, or reward someone simply because they're around. These heavy feelings can lead to the bending or flat-out ignoring of boundaries simply to feel normal again and to be accepted and to feel loved. If you're the first or only person in your circle to graduate, to break six figures, to own property, etc., you may feel isolated in your feelings of loneliness associated with the pressure to be for everyone else what you haven't even fully stepped into for yourself.

Survivors' remorse is a reaction to financial trauma. The reaction may show up as money avoidance, where you give away money or overspend on others because you don't feel you deserve it or have negative feelings about having it. It can show up as money worship, where no amount of money is enough for you because you've taken on the burden of caring for others' financial needs. As you try to use money to bridge the identities of a version of you that survived what others may not have, and a version of you trying to thrive, it's more important than ever not only to have boundaries, but to stand by them completely.

What Financial Boundaries Look Like

Financial boundaries for you may fall in one of the following categories based on this text:

- Internal boundaries
- Relational boundaries
- Situational boundaries

Internal boundaries look like creating a stop on nonessential spending by planning for it. In budgeting language this looks like creating a category that you contribute to for recreational expenses. These are wants, not needs, and they are intended purely and exclusively for you. When you establish the cadence and amount for this category, you adhere to it, allowing you to maintain discipline while ensuring that you enjoy the fruits of your labor. Once this allotment is depleted, you wait until the next allotment, and you do it all over again. If you don't spend all of your previous allotment, congratulations! You now have a greater allotment the next cycle. Setting spending limits, having budgeting clarity, and checking in with yourself emotionally to ensure you aren't overspending are all positive indicators of strong internal boundaries.

Relational boundaries look like practicing scripting and communication tactics to ensure your relationships understand your financial goals and obligations without feeling like they don't matter to you. Communication is a big part of establishing relational boundaries, and you may create rules for relationships and money, like, you don't loan money to family members, or you have a separate savings you contribute to for family emergencies that once depleted is as far as your generosity goes. Of course, you can create exceptions around this, but the idea is that your relational boundaries are dictated and reinforced by you. These boundaries can even extend into your estate planning and intended gift giving. If you want a certain criteria met in order for your descendants and relatives to access any inherited money, you can have that codified in your will.

Situational boundaries may be a mix of relational and internal pressures based on cultural events like weddings and baby showers, religious gatherings, and vacations. Many times these events feel like a necessity based on proximity, relationship history, or familial norms. These events often come with a price tag or expected contribution financially that can derail or depress your financial goals. Situational boundaries may be the most difficult to enforce due to the seemingly once in a lifetime nature for many of them.

To be clear, I'm not recommending that if you skip out on these events this makes you financially responsible. I'm only suggesting that it's important to recognize where your values lie in relation to your financial goals and how these categories can influence your behavior if you are not prepared.

Somatic Boundary Awareness

How do you know when a boundary is crossed? Pay attention to your body when you feel a boundary being crossed. Does your heart rate go up in panic? Do you feel pressure in your shoulders or back? Do you feel heat or numbness in your chest or extremities? Do you start to fidget your hands?

Practice a body scan when you are faced with enforcing a financial boundary like being asked for money or dealing with guilt from saying no.

Reinforcing Financial Boundaries in Real Life

Having prepared responses can make asserting boundaries less daunting, although it may not completely eliminate the discomfort in doing so. Going back to the three-part Financial Boundary Setting Framework, your boundaries should be rooted in your safety. That means that your values, goals, and subsequent behaviors all exist to lay down a foundation of safety, to build on that safety, and to protect that safety. When that safety is threatened you may feel the fight/flight/freeze/fawn responses begin to surface and by now can not only recognize what they feel like, but regulate those feelings to recognize that your boundaries exist to protect you. Here are some example scripts you can use as inspiration for scripts you create on your own.

You can use these scripts in response to **requests for money**:

"Can we talk about other ways I can support you besides money? Maybe we can brainstorm together."

"I care about you, but I'm not in a position to lend money right now."

"I don't loan more than I can afford to lose."

You can use this script in response to **an invitation to spend money out**:

"I'm on a budget and can't join for an expensive dinner but let's catch up in a way that doesn't involve spending money. Dinner at my house?"

"I only spend $200/month on eating out."

You can use this script in response to **a family emergency**:

"I've made a commitment to my own financial goals and can't contribute right now. How can I offer emotional support?"

"I've contributed what I could to a family fund but I also have limits I need to stick to so I don't create new problems for me."

And as a reminder, in all instances, "no" is a complete sentence that doesn't require elaboration.

My advice is to practice creating your own scripts for situations you encounter that align with your values, goals, and feelings of safety. As you create and practice these scripts, remember that you aren't abandoning your community by holding boundaries; you're modeling a new blueprint. You're creating culture and offering it up for anyone who is willing to accept it.

Working with boundaries keeps you rooted in sustainability, dignity, and shared healing.

Chapter 14

Building a Financial Support System

"Much of the wealth that we need is right before our eyes. If we aggregate, we can see it. If we work together, we can acquire it or create it. We are simply blind to our own wealth potential."

—*Claud Anderson, PowerNomics*

In my 2019 Tedx Talk I end with a clear call to action—build a team! I recognized then somehow that before the credentials, the notoriety, becoming trauma aware, or stumbling across the phrase *financial trauma* that one of the key components to financial empowerment and financial healing was building community. In fact, the original talk title was "Financial Empowerment Is a Team Sport." Throughout much of this book I've talked to you about personal transformation and your reaction to the systems, expectations, and isolation that causes your nervous system to flag down danger or a threat. While I believe that if you do the work this book suggests in following the 3E™ framework, you will be well on your way to financial healing, I'd be remiss if I didn't dedicate an entire chapter to financial healing by way of active engagement in building, preserving, and leveraging community.

It seems almost counterintuitive to discuss money through the lens of communal groups and practices, and when I say "counter-intuitive," what I really mean is anti-American. In sharing my work I've come across rebuttals not to the efficacy in what I point out or recommend, but to the "Marxist" and socialist nature of my call. Yet the instigators to these calls always seem to fit a familiar arche-type. While I do occasionally field a curve ball from someone who looks like me articulating their discomfort on my highlighting the interconnectedness of systemic and racial trauma on financial access and subsequent behavior, I recognize that painting capital-ism as the villain is anything but safe. It's disruptive and revealing and ironically puts those who subscribe to it in a dysregulated state that triggers the same fight-or-flight responses I discuss through-out this book. Challenging capitalism as a financial educator and a financial influencer is relatively novel. But as I've shared many times over, capitalism seeks to isolate, and the only way to combat isolation is by building community.

Revisiting the Myth of Individualism

Americans pride themselves on the idea that their success is built as a result of their individual efforts. There's a cultural fanaticism on the "self-made" entrepreneur who bootstrapped their way to millions. This portrayal, however, is just propaganda that perpetu-ates the myth of individualism while the sinister truths of nepo-tism, the exploitation of cheap or free labor, marginalization, and theft fuel capitalism and the idea of a free market. It dangles the carrot safely wrapped up in metaphors of success, riches, love, and respect while simultaneously upholding the values of workaholism, hustle culture, and tolerance for toxicity and abuse all while the wealth is funneled upward. Should you falter, stumble, or other-wise display your natural fatigue, you will be criticized and ridi-culed as a moral and personal failure. Should you somehow succeed, know that those above you have made multiple times your success based on your labor and the labor of people like you—peers, colleagues, and countless others whose contributions go unseen and underpaid. The truth is, those at the top may have worked hard for a time to get there, but they didn't get there alone. In every case, they were successful because they had a community— seen or unseen, known or unknown—that they were able to draw from.

Am I saying it's impossible to grind your way to wealth? Emphatically no! There are many examples of determined individuals who, despite great odds, have achieved financial success. These examples should be celebrated, should be embraced, and studied for their ability to navigate these obstacles. What I am saying is that you shouldn't have to be extraordinary to achieve safety. That personal agency and community support is the winning recipe, not one or the other. I'm also saying that leaning into community means curating it—structuring it with an agreed-upon cultural code that maintains safety and healing within its walls. Not all communities are safe, and not all communities—even the ones you come from—want to see you win. This chapter is about helping you to curate community as a healing superpower and as a wealth-building amplifier.

Community As a Trauma Recovery Tool

Trauma research now supports what indigenous cultures have long understood: there is healing power in community. As Bessel Van Der Kolk notes in *The Body Keeps the Score*, "Numerous studies of disaster response around the globe have shown that social support is the most powerful protection against becoming overwhelmed by stress and trauma" (p. 81).

I've experienced this firsthand when I almost allowed my own financial trauma to negatively influence a purchasing decision to buy a home I was already prequalified for based on a fear of it not working out. This might have at the time seemed irrational; however, it was rooted in the very same experiences I open this book discussing: fear, shame, and a perceived lack of security.

My community at that time consisted of friends and trusted professionals who had been through the process already, who knew what to expect, and who reassured me that they would be there to support me when or if I ever needed them to. I think it's important to note that at that moment in time, those who were so central to my community neither looked like me nor shared my painful experiences. They are also no longer part of any active community with me today. I share this detail because community takes many shapes and forms. It doesn't need to be static for it to be effective. You may see a therapist until you resolve what you went to them to resolve. You may hire a coach to teach you a skill or overcome a roadblock. You may require a professional or a friend for one version of yourself at a given time that may not serve you as another version of yourself during another time. And some people become fixtures in your life for the rest of your life, and all of these instances are okay.

I specifically reference instances where the communities you curate are not part of your immediate family or bloodline because in addition to working against individualist culture, you may be carrying a collective financial trauma. Examining the intergenerational transmission of trauma and epigenetic expression discussed in earlier chapters, sometimes you simply won't find healing at home. That's not to say you can't connect with your inherited community—your family—and collectively heal, just that your healing should align in time and frequency with those actively engaged in the healing process or who want to see you healed.

As Van der Kolk notes elsewhere, "Trauma, whether it is the result of something done to you or something you yourself have done, almost always makes it difficult to engage in intimate relationships" (p. 13).

In other words, trauma doesn't just wound—it isolates. The very tool we need to heal exists in our community yet it becomes harder to reach. So if those around you are still deep in their own trauma cycles, you may find yourself repeating patterns instead of rewriting them.

Van der Kolk puts it plainly, "Social support is not the same as merely being in the presence of others. The critical issue is reciprocity; being truly heard and seen by the people around us, feeling that we are held in someone else's mind and heart" (p. 81).

The unfortunate truth is that if you're reading this book, your family is likely experiencing the effects of their own financial trauma. You can invite them into the healing process, yes—but you can't force it. Your healing deserves to happen in spaces where you are seen, heard, and held. Even if that space has to be built from scratch.

Reclaiming Collectivism

I've described how trauma isolates and how community heals, but it's not enough to seek and find emotional safety in community healing. After all, the big draw to the individualistic nature of capitalism is economic sustainability. Collectivist cultures, both historically and globally, are rooted in shared resources, mutual aid, and interdependence. Even within our own political and economic systems we see reflections of these ideas and ideologies played out. It's just dressed up as corporate bailouts, Social Security, and bureaucratic government assistance programs. Look, I'm not trying to turn you into a communist—but in the context of financial healing, collectivism is the game being played on every level but yours. It's not about abandoning personal responsibility; it's about refusing to carry the burden alone.

How many times have you heard the saying "It's not what you know but who you know"? or that "your network is your net worth"? That's collectivism. Just because your individual name is in the headlines doesn't mean that you aren't representing a collective interest, ideology, or group of people. By nature, human beings are tribal and communal. These are fundamental facts to the way we are socialized and advertised to. The individual is a myth, and the individual will perish.

Dr. Claud Anderson, in PowerNomics, argues that economic empowerment within Black communities requires a shift from individual accumulation to group economics—circulating wealth among trusted networks to create long-term systemic power. In the United States, we've seen how various immigrant and marginalized communities have historically used pooled resources, community lending circles, and intra-community commerce to protect against exclusion and build wealth. It's not a new concept, just one wrapped in the trauma of loss and destruction. There is pain, shame, and anger—rightful anger—associated with that trauma, but now is the time for healing. This looks like the pooling of resources, intentional collaboration, and trusting that your community's win is also your win. This requires healing on an individual and communal level. It requires exposure, education, and execution.

Where Individualism says you have to work hard and be extraordinary to win, Collectivism says your healing, safety, and wealth should not require you to be extraordinary or alone.

Remember, it's only lonely at the top because you're not supposed to be there alone.

> - *Individualism: Self-reliance, competition, ownership, secrecy, burnout, overconsumption, shame.*
> - *Collectivism: interdependence, cooperation, shared resources, transparency, rest, distribution of resources, healing.*

Collectivist practices don't have to look very different from what you may see or practice already within your networks. If you've ever participated in a mastermind group, joined a professional association, crowd funded, participated in lending circles or savings clubs, participated in sou-sous,[1] etc., you've engaged in collectivist practices.

The lens by which you approach these practices is the major difference you will notice in naming it. For example, ask yourself the next time you engage in networking, are you looking solely to find or create an opportunity for you or are you looking to share an opportunity with someone else? If your motives are solely you-focused, then that likely will come across energetically, and people may be turned off or shut down around you.

Another example of a collectivist practice would be if you and a group of friends pooled resources to buy a business or piece of real estate. Now you have shared ownership, shared up-front cost, and shared profit. When I started shaking the generational trauma chain and purchased my house, I bought a duplex. I engaged in collectivism by having my mom and stepfather move into one of the units while I occupied the other. They were able to save on housing costs, and I was able to save on my mortgage. Several years later, due to the decrease in housing costs, they were able to purchase their own home. I sat in awe one day as I left my mom's house looking at the three cars in her driveway reflecting back to a time when we had no house, no car, and an eviction notice on the door of the apartment we occupied, wondering if we were going to be kicked out.

Group Economics

Throughout this book I've been intentional about the names and sources I've included to help illustrate my points and anchor my positions. One of the voices you've gotten to hear from the most is that of Dr. Claud Anderson. In his book *PowerNomics*, Anderson

---

[1] Sou-sous are informal and communal-based savings and lending circles that are popular in West Africans and Caribbeans practiced among trusted family and friend groups. Not to be confused with scams like the Blessing Loom or pyramid schemes.

lays out a national plan to empower Black America that includes group economics. I believe the focus on group economics and his plan is the collective and communal compliment to the personal healing transformation I introduce in this book. Where this book provides the internal recalibration and boundary setting needed to heal, Anderson offers the infrastructure required to sustain that healing at scale. As such, I'm going to mention his 12 economic action steps as a demonstration of how community can be both a buffer and amplifier in healing and building wealth, particularly for Black people (Anderson, 2001).

- Step 1: Create an alternative economy with Black communities.
- Step 2: Dominate business ownership and management where Black people are the majority consumer population.
- Step 3: Focus on wealth building and restoring the economic intent of the original civil rights laws.
- Step 4: Counter the "brain drain" with businesses that aggressively attract Black talent from schools, the government, and corporate America.
- Step 5: Establish solid "root" businesses within Black communities.
- Step 6: Construct vertical businesses and industries that control all processes from raw resources in markets within and outside of Black communities.
- Step 7: Stop the "capital drain" out of Black communities. In other words, "buy Black, but sell to anyone."
- Step 8: Attract semi-finished products into Black communities for value-added manufacturing, processing, and assembling.
- Step 9: Promote the competitive advantages of Black communities.
- Step 10: Establish "safe business zones" based upon a code of conduct in Black business communities.
- Step 11: Amass "vision" capital and wealth through community-based financial efforts.
- Step 12: Establish international economic alliances and marketing agreements between Black America, Black Africa, and Caribbean nations.

Anderson's 12-step action plan may, to some, look daunting; however, in his book he explains what each action step looks like and why it matters. For the purpose of maintaining my framing under this execution phase of the book, I will not go into detail on his 12 economic action steps and rather encourage you to focus on the healing aspects of community building so that you can address your own financial trauma. My only caution comes from a conversation I had with Resmaa Menakem, author of *My Grandmother's Hands*, while I was writing this book. He said to me that "you cannot create individual solutions to communal wounds." Personal agency in your financial healing is possible and requires work, but the traumas you navigate—financial and otherwise—aren't just yours. That is why healing must happen on both personal and collective levels—because the trauma didn't begin with you.

How can you practice group economics today without owning a corporation or organizing a national movement? You can start small, start local, and start with intention right where you are, right now.

Buy from within your community intentionally. Amazon makes enough money, and while I'm not Amazon shaming, you can choose a local or culturally aligned business to support monthly. Your dollar is a vote. Thinking about philanthropy and angel investing or accredited investing? That's great. I'll share more on that in Chapter 17.

You can also barter and share skills. Who said you have to spend money to exchange value? You can set up a skill exchange with friends to learn, accomplish tasks, and test each other's products/services/skills before you go to market.

You can invest together in a savings challenge, stock club, or crowd-funded real estate portfolio. Just make sure you understand the intricacies of compliance and legal requirements with entity formation and reporting.

You can create visibility pipelines, masterminds (paid or unpaid), and organize community info sessions. Group economics doesn't have to be just you spending your money with other businesses; you deserve to get paid too. Offer your skills and services to your community marketplace so others have an opportunity to practice group economics by also supporting you.

These aren't just financial acts—they're cultural and communal ones. Every time you choose community over competition, reciprocity over extraction, and healing over hustle, you're writing a new chapter in your financial healing story.

Building a Financial Support System

Now that we've dismantled individualism, reclaimed collectivism, and spotlighted the economic power in having community, you need to actually build one. Your financial support system is going to comprise five primary categories—where you may see some overlap between multiple.

- Accountability partners
- Professional guides
- Peer networks
- Vendors
- Collaborators

Accountability partners are people who hold you accountable to your goals—ideally without shame. They don't have to be further ahead than you and will likely consist of mentors, trusted friends, family members, or a partner who wants to see you win.

Professional guides are your financial therapists, coaches, counselors, planners, tax professionals, etc. They are often credentialed, experienced, and qualified. They understand your values and should be trauma informed.

Peer networks are people who are in the trenches with you—your tribe. They may be teaching you, learning from you, or sharing resources with you. You might bump into them in online communities, as members of an association, at conferences, or through social networking.

Vendors are service providers who may or may not offer guidance beyond providing you a service. Think real estate agent, business broker, bankers, lawyers, etc.

Collaborators are people who are invested in helping you build for the future. They may be customers, supporters, business partners, or beneficiaries. They understand that your win is their win and they are willing to build with you.

Think of the five people you interact with most and where they might fall in this list. If the answer is nowhere, that's okay. These people serve a purpose that is not part of your financial support system. However, it is important to find people and groups who can fill these buckets not just so that you can improve your financial health but so that you can improve your financial healing, so that you don't feel misunderstood or isolated, and so that you can practice culture change and financial boundary setting in a safe and values-aligned environment.

That is the power of community.

Chapter 15

Financial Therapy and Alternative Healing

When I was a child, I would occasionally stay at my grandfather's house and wake up in the morning to the sound of drums. My brother, my uncle, and I had a ritual: we would get up, pray, meditate, and do some form of physical exercise. We would help prepare breakfast, everyone with their own tasks, and later in the day we would have rec time where my grandfather would take us out to a park for an hour or so to just run around and burn off energy.

I don't claim to be an expert on somatic healing practices, but I do know that I've been engaged in some form or another for most of my life. My grandfather would tell us that any time we were hurt, sick, anxious, or tired to "summon chi,"[1] where we would do a deep inhale, hold, and exhale accompanied by hand movement to direct the flow of chi throughout our bodies. At the time I was too young to understand the concept of chi or energy and too young to understand what I was doing when I would sit down in

---

[1] Chi is the vital energy or energy flow recognized in many Eastern healing practices.

a lotus pose to meditate, to understand my grandfather's wisdom in taking us to the park to burn off the energy of the day. I didn't understand the nuance of healing, communication, and energy that existed by listening to and sometimes accompanying the rhythm of African drums—but I did absorb it and internalize it.

As I grew older, I noticed that I used some of these exercises to calm down and regulate my nervous system in times of frustration, in times of anxiety or panic, or when I was experiencing emotional chaos. I never thought that I would talk about these activities and exercises through the lens of financial healing, but through all of the research that I've done in understanding trauma and how trauma exists in the body, one thing I've learned for certain is that talk therapy alone doesn't necessarily address the trauma that's in your body—it just gives it a name. I've learned that somatic practices not only help to regulate your nervous system during times of stress or the trauma responses but also allow you to slow things down internally just enough so that you can control your reaction to your current environment.

Years after my grandfather's introduction to these practices I experienced my own battles with depression and anxiety and found safety and regulation in wing chun kung fu, a form of martial arts. Many of the practices and philosophies related to chi, mindfulness, breathwork, and movement were echoed in wing chun. I was drawn to martial arts because martial arts had been a part of my life for most of my life. It was always emphasized that I should be able to defend myself physically, but I hadn't considered the other benefits associated with this practice.

Somatic healing is one of the methods I've found—through research and experience—to be the most effective in metabolizing trauma. In this chapter, I'll walk you through a range of healing modalities for financial trauma: from financial therapy and traditional therapy interventions to somatic practices, affirmations, breathwork, and beyond.

If there is one chapter in this book I want everyone to read, it's this one. Healing doesn't take one shape. Healing looks like whatever we need it to look like, and the tools introduced in this section are tools you can use to initiate healing from multiple lenses that honor your body, your spirit, and your mind.

What Is Financial Therapy?

The Financial Therapy Association (FTA) defines *financial therapy* as a process informed by both therapeutic and financial competencies that help people think, feel, communicate, and behave differently with money to improve overall well-being through evidence-based practices and interventions.[2] At the time of this writing, I'm both an active member and committee chair on the board of directors for the FTA. I unite with this definition of financial therapy while also acknowledging that financial therapy carries definitions outside of the Financial Therapy Association's that suggest it's merely a specialization of psychotherapy, a pseudoscience, or simply "any act, hobby, task, program, etc., that relieves tension" (according to Dictionary.com) related to money.

People come to financial therapy as financial professionals, mental health professionals, a mixture of both, or neither, with the goal of helping to improve their clients relationship with money. My approach to financial therapy is multifaceted. With a financial base coming from financial services and financial counseling, I understand the nuances of financial systems, their products and services, and consumer behavior within those systems.

Through a trauma responsive lens, I understand the unseen and often unnamed variables that prompt both voluntary and involuntary responses to financial trauma—that trigger financial anxiety, financial stress, and money disorders.

---

[2] See https://financialtherapyassociation.org.

Through a socio-cultural and experience-based lens I understand the impact of systems, politics, culture, history, and oppression that shape the narratives you hold about yourself internally and in relation to others.

While I use the title *financial therapist* to define my work, it may be more appropriate to refer to me as a financial activist, a financial healer, and a financial abolitionist. With financial therapy being an emerging field, however, I've observed a great openness to innovation, social and economic justice, diversity of thought and experience, peer review, and research-based assessments of the lived experiences of all people. Occupying space as a financial therapist for me means that I get to influence the field of financial therapy as it grows by contributing thought leadership, lived experiences, and directional change while also learning the intervention styles, vocabulary, and research, and building community while pushing the field forward.

Financial therapy seeks to merge mental health and financial behavior by acknowledging that both impact each other—a departure from conservative perspectives on finance.

Financial therapy is not a fad or flavor of the month. Financial therapy is here to stay.

Within financial therapy I've observed my peers pulling from different modalities to help address a spectrum of challenges with clients that include attachment theory, cognitive behavioral theory, EMDR, internal family systems, narrative therapy, Reiki, and more. Because this is not a book with a broad financial therapy focus and rather exclusively focuses on financial trauma, I will only be highlighting what I feel is necessary to address financial trauma as I've presented and defined it. If you're interested in financial therapy broadly, I invite you to learn more by visiting the FTA website at financialtherapyassociation.org and by reading *Financial Therapy: Theory, Research, and Practice* (Klontz et al., 2015).

Top-Down Regulation and Mindfulness

In Chapter 7 I introduced the triune brain as a conceptual framework for understanding the evolutionary responses hardwired into the brain that trigger the fight-or-flight response. If you recall, at the top of the brain is our most recently evolved portion of the brain—the neocortex—which houses the prefrontal cortex in the frontal lobe and is responsible for rational thought, logic, regulating emotion, restoring balance, and aborting the stress response. Top-down regulation is a behavioral approach to leveraging your prefrontal cortex to change the threat detection by essentially sending messages based on logic that indicate you are safe or what you are perceiving as a threat is actually not as big a threat as you may have originally thought. Bessel Van der Kolk uses the analogy of a smoke alarm going off while cooking a steak to illustrate this. Your limbic system, as the smoke alarm reacts to the smoke and yells "Fire!" Your prefrontal cortex, however, says, "I'm not in danger; I'm cooking a steak. Let me open a window or turn on a fan to dissipate some of the smoke so the alarm stops going off." Essentially, this is what occurs when employing a practice like mindfulness.

Top-down regulation can involve mindfulness practices as simple as yoga to a more complex relationship with a cognitive behavioral therapist. It's important to note that top-down regulation and mindfulness do not heal past trauma, but it does allow you to analyze and assess the impact of past trauma on present-day beliefs and decision-making. This is especially useful in instances involving financial anxiety where you are reacting to a financial issue or threat that has not yet—and may not ever—come to pass. One of my favorite quick mindfulness techniques involves grounding myself so I can feel my feet flat on the floor or in a meditative pose with my legs crossed and going through each one of my five senses while asking myself the question "What do I see, feel, taste, hear, smell, right now?" By bringing myself into the present moment, I can remind myself of and more importantly recognize my safety in the moment before taking further action or deciding to disengage with whatever triggered me. Other examples of mindfulness include journaling, martial arts, exercise, grounding, and prayer. Top-down regulation involves strengthening the capacity of the watchtower to monitor your body's sensations. Bottom-up regulation involves recalibrating the autonomic nervous system (Van Der Kolk, 2015).

"Dear Money" exercise: During my Trauma of Money certification, I participated in an activity led by one of the instructors where I wrote a letter to money. Money could take on the shape or attribute of whoever or whatever I needed it to. Write a letter to money about what it represents to you, what it allows you to do, how it hurt you, how it helps you, or any other interaction that comes to mind. Reflect on your feedback alone or in community.

Bottom-Up Regulation and the Vagus Nerve

I've discussed the fight-or-flight response as something being triggered in the brain that has whole-body implications. Known as the sympathetic nervous system (SNS), heart rate, respiration, and blood flow are activated in the fight-or-flight response. While this is a largely accepted conceptual framework, by and large an incomplete one. Our human response to real or perceived threats is often a whole-body response that enlists your vagus nerve, a cranial nerve that runs from the brainstem to the lungs, heart, stomach, and intestines.

Polyvagal theory, introduced by Stephen Porges, explains how the vagus nerve influences nervous system response to safety, danger, and social engagement. It distinguishes between the ventral vagal system, which supports social engagement and safety, and the dorsal vagal system, which governs immobilization, withdrawal, and shutdown, often described as the freeze response.

Perhaps most significantly, polyvagal theory acknowledges that humans are attuned to emotional shifts in the people around them that signal safety and danger and speaks to the coregulation of emotional responses between humans. Polyvagal theory provides evidence of the healing power of community through emotional co-regulation.

The vagus nerve is involved in that gut feeling you feel when you think to turn left instead of right or to cross the street because something doesn't feel right. It's the butterflies you feel in your gut when you are nervous or excited. This matters because your body's ability to sense, respond to, and regulate these cues is essential to healing financial trauma, because if your body doesn't feel safe, your mind can't focus on money, planning, or possibility beyond survival mode.

In bottom-up regulation, rather than rationalizing your safety, you are recalibrating your body's response to a real or imagined threat. If that threat is difficult to identify as it often is related to financial trauma—think about the smoke alarm going off but you can't find the source of the smoke—you can't rationalize your safety beyond a learned helplessness or acceptance that there is nothing wrong and that the problem is you.

Bottom-up regulation can involve breathwork, humming, rocking, drumming, chanting, movement, dancing, crying, shouting, and other forms of somatic healing. While some of these practices have been acquired over time, many are indigenous in nature going back thousands of years. Modern-day manifestations in music and popular culture like the creation of the Blues, church choirs, reclaiming African dance, step dancing, and drumming are just echoes of the innate ways your ancestors learned to channel pain into healing. These echoes not only still work but are needed ingredients in financial healing.

Reiki and Somatic Healing

Somatic healing has shown up in my life long before I had the language for it—and now I know why talk therapy alone wasn't enough. Yet, as I sat down to write this book, it weighed on me that I was offering an incomplete solution as a practitioner. I could walk my clients through the 3E™ Framework right on through the Execution phase, but I didn't have any direct experience with walking a client through a somatic healing intervention specifically focused on financial trauma.

In exploring alternative healing modalities for financial trauma, I had the opportunity to interview my good friend Steven M. Hughes, a financial therapist and Reiki master teacher. Steven integrates financial psychology with energy healing through a practice known as Reiki to address deep-seated emotional and energetic blocks that often underlie financial distress. To go deeper, I didn't just interview Steven—I became the client. That session unlocked the breakthroughs I described in Chapter 12. I share this because I want you to know that even financial therapists can benefit from financial therapy and that not only am I talking the talk, but I'm also walking the walk.

During the interview with Steven I asked him what Reiki was and what physical and energetic manifestations of trauma he observes in the clients he works with. "Reiki is a healing practice preserved in Japan that helps aid in relaxation and stress reduction by balancing energy centers in our body known as chakras. This balancing has an impact on our auric, physical and ethereal bodies as the energy healing goes through the chakras," Steven says. He emphasizes that Reiki was preserved in Japan because energy healing has been part of our community for thousands of years and that once preserved, it began to move west.

On physical manifestations of trauma Steven notes that the same locations where you experience nervousness and excitement—usually felt in your core such as chest, stomach, and back—will be the same areas you will feel the physical manifestation of trauma. He notes that "it's energy in your body, and energy can't be created or destroyed" and can get stuck in the body.

Steven highlights and explains what chakras are, where they are located, and what affiliation they have to our sense of self. He shares that the first three chakras can be blocked or unbalanced causing or due to associated fear, shame, and guilt:

- The root chakra (at the base of the spine responsible for our sense of survival and groundedness)
- The sacral chakra (in the lower abdomen responsible for the reproductive system, emotions, and creativity)
- The solar plexus chakra (between the belly button and rib cage responsible for self-esteem and personal power)

"If your chakras are clear, you have more space to have clarity in decision-making," he says.

I asked Steven about the role of somatic healing in financial therapy and whether it should be a non-negotiable part of financial healing. Steven said that the goal of somatic healing practices is connecting our mind and body so that we can operate from a whole place. "We are marketed to, to separate our mind and our body," and Steven says that we may then make a decision to feel in control and safe from this place of separation. "Reiki brings your energetic bodies together. If these bodies are together, you can make better decisions."

Steven shares that in some sessions with clients he's had their ancestors present and that energetic trauma transferred across multiple generations can be unblocked and addressed. "I believe that money is more about thoughts and emotions than it is about math and numbers," he says. Steven believes it is mandatory for somatic healing to be part of the conversation around systemic change like reparations, housing, income, and health disparities because "When we talk about these things we talk about something owed or something missing. Trauma keeps you from being your whole self and somatic healing helps you become whole. Whole people can have whole solutions."

Steven notes that people may view somatic healing as an individualistic practice that just serves the person. He says that "if you become more of a whole person, you can help the people around you see what a whole person looks like and continue down their journey to become a whole person. If you are going through somatic healing yourself, you will have a positive impact on the world."

Both Reiki and somatic healing practices like breathwork, body scans, grounding, and centering, etc., address what words alone cannot by unlocking trapped trauma energy in the body. What I like about Reiki is that it bridges the gap between mind, body, and spirit to get the three working as one.

Financial Genogram

A genogram is a tool used by therapists and healthcare professionals focused on money that can help visually illustrate your generational family relationships through financial attitudes and behaviors. It's a visual representation of behaviors, beliefs, and patterns that may have caused or may be the result of trauma.

This matters because it reveals inherited scarcity or consumption patterns, identifies the root of certain money beliefs, and bridges talk therapy and somatic insight by offering a map of where money wounds might have originated.

You can build a simple genogram by drawing a family tree of you, your parents, and grandparents. Next to each person add details about their known money habits, events, and the emotional undertones they shared around money. If there was a forced sale (or theft) of property, an unpaid life insurance policy, family disputes over inheritance, gambling, alcoholism or drugs, etc., document these events to the associated branch of the family tree.

When you have a visual representation of the behaviors and financial patterns of your family, ask yourself where there are repeating patterns, what emotions arise while doing this activity, and what somatic responses show up in your body.

Affirmations and Rituals as Rewiring Tools

Affirmations may have previously been dismissed as pseudoscience or wishful thinking without scientific backing, but neuroscience research supports what indigenous cultures have long known, the words we speak can rewire our brains. In *Becoming Supernatural*, Dr. Dispenza explains that "what you put your attention on and mentally rehearse over and over again not only becomes who you are from a biological perspective, it also determines your future" (p. 37). In Chapter 12, I pull from Dr. Dispenza's work to guide you through visualizing your financial healing through a future state experience, encouraging you to approach it as if it has already happened. The science supports that future-self visualization and repetitive affirmations anchor and strengthen neural pathways that lead to lasting changes in thought, behavior, and biology.

You make affirmations daily. You were socialized to do so from a young age. When someone says "Good morning," you reply in kind. When someone sneezes, you might tell them "Bless you." When it's your or someone else's birthday, you repeat "Happy birthday." You sing your favorite songs, repeat lines from movies, or tell yourself things like "You aren't good with money" or "You're broke until payday." When you acknowledge how repetitive sayings become affirmations and unintentionally rewire your brain, you can go from unintentional sayings to intentional ones that bring you closer to financial health, safety, and security.

Dispenza emphasizes the power of combining thought with emotion. He discusses elevated emotions like gratitude and love as anchoring to the visualizations and affirmations we project. It's not enough to just say or think about it. You have to feel the outcomes you seek. You have to actually feel safe. This perspective aligns with the concept of neuroplasticity—the brain's ability to reorganize itself by forming new neural connections.

In the realm of financial healing, this approach is particularly potent. By affirming statements like, I am financially secure, or abundance flows to me, you can begin to shift your mindset from scarcity to abundance, which creates a path for you to make healthier financial behaviors.

Indigenous and Decolonized Healing Practices

One of the greatest gifts my grandfather gave to me was to teach me how to acknowledge and call on my ancestors. He often described them as if they were in the room with us, involving them in family discussions and learning experiences. When we did something wrong or dishonest, my grandfather would have us apologize to everyone in the home for that wrongdoing and ask for forgiveness. He had pictures of different ancestors on the walls of his apartment that we would also apologize to and acknowledge as part of our family rituals. As a child, it didn't feel weird to me because it was so normalized. There were strong connections between my self-esteem and that ancestral acknowledgment. For most of my life, the ancestral realm seemed conceptual and separate. Despite the normalization of ancestral reverence, it wasn't until my grandfather transitioned out of this life to become an ancestor himself that I truly felt connected to them through my connection to him.

Ancestral veneration has existed long before therapy as a healing practice and source of guidance. The engagement of our ancestors is wrapped in mysticism and a firm side eye from Western values and academics that uphold empirical data as the standard for measuring efficacy and success in healing. Yet, with the increase in focus and acknowledgment of intergenerational trauma transfer and epigenetic impact, we can point to data that validates our ancestors' pain and with that, their gifts of wisdom, resilience, and survival.

To treat modern healing methods as the only credible route is not just inaccurate, it's colonial. Indigenous practices, like ancestral veneration, offer powerful and time-tested ways to address trauma, grief, the disconnection that comes with individualism, and blockages that impact our relationships with money.

In financial trauma work, this can look like acknowledging inherited beliefs, behaviors, and burdens, and consciously choosing to transform them with the help of your ancestors. Shame, scarcity, and avoidance behaviors may not have started with you, but you can work to transform it.

I'm not sharing this to force a choice between therapy lenses and tradition—I'm recommending they both be integrated.

Drumming circles, energetic healing practices, working with sound, nature, or movement are ancestral technologies designed to regulate the nervous system, shift internal energy, and help to heal and build community. Decolonized healing practices belong in the conversation around financial healing.

Putting It into Practice

Financial healing is not one size fits all. It's layered, embodied, and deeply personal. This chapter offered a range of approaches from financial therapy, top-down and bottom-up regulation, ancestral veneration, and neuroscience. This section demonstrates how healing requires you to engage the mind, body, and spirit; it's not just "more financial literacy." Because we are in the execution phase I want to offer you exercises you can try right now from each section. Some will be easier to do than others. Some will require you to work with someone else. Make them your own regular parts of your journey. Whatever you do, just take action.

Financial Therapy

You can find a financial therapist through the FTA website and directory, word-of-mouth referrals, social media, and online searches. It's important to understand that financial therapists come with different backgrounds and educational bases. If you are looking for one who is more mental health leaning, then ask about their credentials and experience. If you are looking for one who is more financially leaning, do the same. Many financial therapists will use or make reference to the KMSI-R to understand and help you understand your money scripts. Here is a narrative prompt for you to work on by yourself:

"What's one financial behavior you'd like to change—and what story do you tell yourself about why you do it?"

Write freely. Don't censor yourself. Focus on awareness and not judgment. Remember the Three Es—this is exposure.

Top-Down Regulation: Grounding

This is my favorite grounding exercise when experiencing anxiety or any kind or guilt.

Find a quiet space and plant your feet on the ground.

Close your eyes and slowly ask yourself:

- What do I see right now?
- What do I feel right now (physical pressure, sensations, etc.) ?
- What do I hear right now?
- What do I smell right now?
- What do I taste right now?

Breathe deeply and evenly between each question; then return to the present moment.

Bottom-Up Regulation: Breathwork and Somatic Movement

Swaying, humming, drumming, and breathwork all help to activate the vagus nerve and calm your nervous system. My favorite breathwork exercise involves box breathing in increasing increments.

Inhale into your stomach with your stomach expanding outward for a count of 3–5.

Hold for a count of 3–5.

Exhale for a count of 3–5.

Then repeat.

If you can, increase the count by one each time until you can't maintain the breath anymore, then work your way down decreasing the count until you reach the original 3–5 count breath.

Reiki and Somatic Healing: Body Scan

According to Steven, you can get attuned to Reiki 1 and 2 to begin practicing Reiki on yourself, or you can book a Reiki session with a Reiki master teacher.

Somatic body scans, however, you can practice on your own. Sit or lie down and close your eyes. Bring awareness to your body from head to toe, envisioning each part of your body as you move from your head to toes. Notice where you feel tension, tightness, or numbness. Make a mental note of these sensations and where they occur. Don't forget to breathe.

Genogram Activity: Money Map

Draw a simple family tree. Note key financial behaviors, traumas, or beliefs passed down. Where are the patterns repeating? Where do you want to interrupt them?

Affirmations

You can create your own affirmations that are personal to your healing journey with money. Remember, it's not enough to just say and repeat the affirmation out loud. You want to embody the feeling of safety, success, healing, etc., that you want to bring into your reality. This is not going to be an overnight activity. Perform this exercise over a protracted period. Make it a ritual.

"I am safe, supported, and have permission to heal."

Ancestral Veneration

As you work through your generational financial traumas, enlist the help and guidance of your ancestors.

As a side note, this is an indigenous practice. If you do not acknowledge or believe in ancestral work, you do not need to engage your ancestors as part of your healing process.

Light a candle. Speak the name of the ancestors you know or those unknown. Thank them for their sacrifice, wisdom, strength, and tools for survival. Ask for their guidance and acceptance as you work to unblock generational trauma. Make note of any sensations, insights, scents, sounds, or visual imagery that come up.

Healing doesn't have to be complicated; it just has to be honest. Pick a practice and start with you, where you are. Slowly and intentionally build on that healing by working with a guide and building community.

You deserve it.

Chapter 16

How to Build a Financial Wellness Program

Congratulations! You've made it through most of this book or you're an ambitious overachiever looking to bridge the financial wellness gap at your company or institution. This chapter is going to look and feel a bit different as it's geared toward HR professionals and organizational change makers looking to build a sustainable and scalable financial wellness solution at their organization. I'm going to walk you through a summary of the 3E™ Framework and my lens on financial wellness.

A few things to note: This is not a facilitator's guide. While I have been generous within the pages of this book, that is a service and tool that comes separately. As such, you can feel free to reach out to me or my team at RahkimSabree.com or partner@rahkimsabree.com to discuss the range of services I offer organizations and executive teams.

Let's get started.

Root Your Program in Financial Trauma Literacy

You do not have to be a financial trauma expert to acknowledge the impact and effects of financial trauma on your workforce. While it can be uncomfortable to acknowledge in some lines of business, generally the financial trauma people are experiencing is an echo of previous trauma being activated by present-day conditions. Leaders of organizations and people should recognize how their leadership styles can trigger financial trauma, and individual contributors should recognize how their experiences with financial trauma can impact their morale, performance, ambitions, and approaches to career development.

Start with education that contextualizes money behavior in trauma, culture, and systemic forces. Before you can teach what to do with money, teach why people do what they do even when it intuitively doesn't make sense. This is why I developed the 3E™ Framework with Exposure being the first E. People often don't recognize the influences of their direct experiences with the concept and application of money, their early observations and programming around money, and generational narratives passed down based on other people's experiences with money on their financial behavior and outlook. They need that lens to understand what to do about it.

Core components of your program should include:

- Introduction to financial trauma with personal, generational, and systemic lenses
- Behavioral finance and money scripts
- Understanding the stress response and physical manifestations of trauma
- Financial literacy
- Financial boundaries and support systems
- Mechanisms for healing

Incorporate the 3E™ Framework
(Exposure, Education, Execution)

The Three E's aren't just a catchy framework put together for easy remembrance. It's been carefully crafted to guide people through their experiences with financial trauma and can be applied through most learning topics and learning styles.

If you examine the three primary learning styles (visual, auditory, and kinesthetic), the Three Es can be delivered through each ensuring maximum reach and cross-over adoption with delivery mediums ranging from storytelling, guided reflection, hands-on application, articles and historical texts, and more.

The Three Es are thematically designed to ease participants into doing instead of passive learning. This can look as follows:

- **Exposure:** Storytelling, money autobiographies, guided reflections, articles, blogs
- **Education:** Scientific data, financial literacy fundamentals, workshops, value alignment
- **Execution:** SMART goal setting, boundary setting, community building, habit building, healing

Narrative work at each stage is important. Participants should be asking themselves, "How does this relate to me? How does this show up for me? What does this mean for me?"

In one engagement with a retail organization, Exposure took the form of money confessions shared via a closed group forum. Education included a series of storytelling paired with trauma-aware literacy modules. Execution looked like direct engagement with me as a financial therapist for a session. The format encouraged engagement, provided data, and validated a need, letting the leadership team know this was desired work, and gave them insights into silent stress points within their teams.

Prioritize Somatic + Emotional Regulation Work

This is a game changer in financial wellness programming. Most financial programs ignore the body, its responses, and how that impacts your relationship with money. Why does it matter? Because dysregulation hijacks logic. Regulated (whole) people make aligned decisions.

It doesn't need to be overcomplicated, just included.

- Breathwork + grounding before and during financial decision-making
- Body scans
- Somatic awareness when boundaries are crossed or retail spending "nudges" occur
- Integration of mindfulness, reiki, or even martial arts and exercise as financial maintenance tools

Focus on Community, Not Individualism

This is a hard but necessary ask of corporate and institutional spaces because the individual is often rewarded. Put into the context of team building and team cohesiveness, though, this isn't a far-off concept to implement. Finance is a taboo topic, but it doesn't have to be. Facilitating conversations on broad financial struggles like employee financial stress and burnout without singling anyone out and creating a space to discuss financial goals can foster an environment where encouragement, community buy-in, and cultural exchange around money take place. This can build community, trust, and humanize relationships between subordinates and superiors who may otherwise feel out of touch due to perceptions around title and take-home pay.

Provide Access to Multiple Healing Modalities

Bringing in your 401(k) plan administrator to discuss investment options within the employee benefit is usually baked into the cost of carrying that plan, but holistic financial wellness is more than understanding employer-sponsored retirement plans and benefit choices. While it may be an additional line item expense for the company, bringing in a qualified financial educator with nothing to sell can make the difference in employee confidence and control of their finances, and can impact employee retention by providing a relevant employee benefit to a well-known employee pain point. The benefit? Employees get to be involved in building their own healing plans. They aren't forced into a cookie-cutter solution for their unique problem.

Examples of professionals that employers hire for one-off or ongoing services include:

- Financial counselors
- Financial therapists
- Financial planners with flat fees
- Financial coaches
- Reiki or energy healers with a focus on financial blockages

Include Culture and Customization

Program design can and should include modular framing so that it can be adapted to the diverse needs of your talent body. Throughout this book I've centered my experience as a Black American; however, the methods and models I introduced can be adjusted, adopted, and articulated through the lens of pretty much anybody. Financial wellness is not one size fits all and should morph based on the needs of the people it's presented to. These can include but are not limited to:

- Affinity groups (e.g., Black professionals, first-generation students, LGBTQ+, military veterans, women leaders, etc.)
- HR departments
- Executive leadership teams
- Middle management
- Frontline workers

For example, a program for first-generation college grads may focus heavily on building foundational literacy and unpacking guilt tied to financial success, while a session with Black professionals may center inherited wealth gaps, cultural money taboos, and the pressure of being the "first or only." LGBTQ+ groups may need space to unpack trauma from financial institutions that have historically excluded or marginalized them. You're not just tweaking language; you're shifting the emotional center of gravity in each room.

It's not enough to say this program works for everyone. While I don't believe we can ever be truly culturally competent, what we can be is culturally aware. Cultural attitudes around money vary drastically, and care should be taken to meet people where they are. In acknowledging the systemic sources of financial trauma, you have to also acknowledge immigrant narratives of wealth and safety, racial wealth gap dynamics, gender and age dynamics, caregiver responsibilities, chronic illness, and more. This is a great opportunity to bring in your diversity, equity, and inclusion (DEI) team or consultant to collaborate.

Implementation

A successful financial wellness program is not going to be plug and play. It's layered, tailored, and strategic. One of the questions I'm asked often by corporate partners is "How do we scale?"

While scale is the ultimate goal, you certainly don't start out that way. Here's my suggested rollout plan:

- **Pilot first:** Start with a focus group or one department to test engagement and collect qualitative feedback. This allows for agile-style adjustments and data collection. This data tells a story.
- **Create internal champions:** Identify and empower team members who already care about financial wellness to serve as advocates and peer leaders. These advocates can later be trained as facilitators of the program in a train-the-trainer feedback loop that rapidly expands the program's adoption. Consider also integrating digital tools to supplement live training. Short videos, self-paced modules, a custom podcast, newsletter, blog, and internal slack groups for peer discussion can provide low barrier entry points and reinforce learning. The goal is not just one-off events but an ongoing cultural shift.
- **Staggered rollouts:** Introduce new components gradually starting first with exposure, then moving into education, and finally offer actionable execution strategies. You should not aim to complete the program in a one- or two-day training. Work involving dislodging and discussing trauma is heavy work, and individuals often need time to process before taking subsequent action.

It's also important to set ethical boundaries. Financial trauma-informed programming is not clinical therapy. Practitioners facilitating this work should be clear about their scope, avoid diagnosing, and have a process to encourage engagement with licensed mental health professionals if participants surface deeper psychological issues. This protects everyone involved and keeps the focus on education and healing, not treatment.

If you want to ensure your implementation sticks, I help organizations launch programs and embed them into the culture.

Measurement Metrics

I know you love data, and we want to measure what matters. There is a bit of abstract fluidity when it comes to financial wellness because we're not specifically checking for total debt eliminated, how many people have a budget, or the average balance of an emergency fund (although you can include and track that data if employees are willing to self-report it). You should want to understand, however, things like how employees feel in relation to money in the workplace. To do that, you'll want to track the following:

- **Pre- and post-survey** data to measure general awareness of topics, employee financial stress, confidence in money management, financial literacy, comfort with engaging financial systems
- **Engagement metrics** that are self-reported (e.g., on a scale of 1–10 this program was relevant to me), and observed engagement (how many people attended, how many people participated, are participants completing follow-up material/ assignments, are participants engaged in peer forums),
- **HR indicators** like improved retention rates, culture shift, general employee engagement and career progression (do participants volunteer to facilitate sessions in the future), etc.

Deeper metrics can be developed and measured at the request of and in partnership with executive leadership. For more executive aligned impact, consider tracking longitudinal metrics like reductions in financial-related absenteeism, healthcare claims tied to stress, or participation in employer-sponsored benefits. You may also tie engagement to productivity tools or performance review insights. While hard to quantify immediately, these data points speak CFO language and tie in the wellness to the bottom line.

Building a financial wellness program shouldn't just be a checkbox for HR; it's a commitment to your team's holistic well-being. By taking a trauma responsive and financial trauma–informed approach that incorporates somatic practices, fosters community support, and includes financial education, you're not only enhancing productivity but also cultivating a resilient and engaged workforce. Don't let this be another initiative that gathers dust; take the first step today. Assess your organization's needs, engage with your employees, and start building a program that truly makes a difference.

Whether you want to launch a pilot or embed trauma-responsive wellness across your entire culture, we're here to help. Don't think of this as outsourcing, but co-creating. Visit RahkimSabree.com or contact partner@rahkimsabree.com to start designing a program that aligns with your people and your mission.

Chapter 17

Philanthropy and Social Responsibility

You may have arrived at a point in your financial journey where you begin finding things to do with your money. You buy new technology, more expensive clothing, you don't have to worry about the bills getting paid, you might even invest—heavily. But something feels like it's missing.

Purpose.

I'm not talking about the obligatory Black tax or giving to your local church. I'm talking about an innate desire to contribute your time and resources to your community in meaningful ways instead of the default contribution to some charity organization where you don't know how your dollars are being used. Almost this entire book focuses on personal transformation and healing—but can you truly heal without helping to heal others?

To some, their bandwidth may only accommodate breaking out of survival and scarcity cycles. I'm not talking to those people in this chapter.

I'm talking to individuals who as part of their healing journey recognize their ability and desire to create security for themselves and others, to create freedom for themselves and others, or to create power for themselves and others.

Financial trauma isn't just an individual burden; it's a societal ailment. It lives in the feelings of disdain you feel when trying not to make eye contact with someone begging for change, not wanting to be thought of as poor in your social groups, the feelings of isolation and pressure you feel when you finally "make it"—because we know making it is subjective and some will never feel that way despite how much financial success they have. It's only fitting after highlighting the systemic and personal roots of financial distress that I conclude by addressing the option and collective responsibility in healing.

Hint: It has less to do with your money than you think!

Overcoming financial trauma requires more than personal budgeting or corporate wellness programs, as you well know. It demands a societal shift where those with resources—be it capital, skills, or networks—actively participate in creating equitable financial ecosystems.

Your healing journey doesn't just stop with you. It continues into the next generation and the generation after that. Your healing lays a foundation for future healed and whole people.

From Scarcity to Surplus

Capitalism thrives on the myth of scarcity and individualism, convincing you that there's not enough to go around, and that in order for you to have it, someone else can't, and vice versa. The truth, however, is that wealth is all around us and that scarcity you feel is manufactured to keep you dysregulated and in a state of fear, shame, and panic so that you continue to seek out ways to regain control and wholeness in your life. Just by acknowledging that there is surplus in the areas where you see lack and shifting your lens on how you define wealth, you can begin to feel an undercurrent of change. Following this program, you can create meaningful change for you and your loved ones. Shifting from scarcity to surplus doesn't mean giving away all of your hard-earned money to those less fortunate. It means shifting your mindset from one of hoarding resources, information, skills, and, yes, money, to one of intentional redistribution in ways that uplift communities. Does that mean you can't get paid for your knowledge? Absolutely not. If you are a knowledge resource and that is how you make your money, then you deserve to be paid for your work. What it does mean is that when you take a step back and examine the values you have been socialized to adopt around access, scarcity, shame, hustle culture, and elitism, you have an opportunity and obligation after reading this book to reassess those values and adopt new ones that seek to serve rather than exploit.

Charity and Community Reinvestment

Charity is often executed through a model of giving that doesn't directly address the root cause of the inequality. If I have a substance abuse problem and you donate some dollar amount to me for the purpose of helping me recover, what's to stop me from taking that dollar amount and blowing it on my substance of choice due to my current condition? You walk away from that experience feeling good about yourself with a post-worthy story to share, and you've given me the tools to my own destruction. Is that your problem? Maybe, maybe not. If your only goal was to give and make yourself feel good about yourself, then you get a gold star, but if you were looking to create meaningful change, not so much. I'm not suggesting that you micro-manage the money you throw into someone's cup who is asking for change to get something to eat. What I'm talking about is the hundreds or thousands of dollars you might sign away to a charitable organization so you can get a tax write-off.

Traditional Charity Looks Like:
- One-time donations with little follow-up
- Funding intermediaries with minimal transparency
- PR-driven giving timed for tax season

Community reinvestment, however, focuses on channeling resources back into communities to build sustainable wealth and opportunities for its inhabitants. Dr. Claud Anderson talks about creating systemic change by organizing, influencing, and owning in our communities. Instead of a one-time donation to a community center, could you consider funding programs that teach essential financial skills, provide micro loans and grants, or support local entrepreneurship? Could you connect with trusted leaders and teachers in that space to ensure the funds are being allocated appropriately? Finding initiatives that address systemic gaps and take trauma responsive approaches to healing could empower communities to build long-term financial resilience, lower or eliminate barriers, and kickstart a feedback loop that continues long after your initial contribution.

Again, community reinvestment doesn't only have to look like giving your money as a resource. I've reinvested in my community by joining boards of nonprofits whose mission I believe in, by donating my time and services to my local library offering discounted workshops and pro bono financial counseling, and by mentoring young men.

Corporate Social Responsibility Reimagined

Traditional corporate social responsibility often centers public relations that may or may not be grounded in genuine impact. It makes investors happy to see corporations engaged in public initiatives that center the people. Stocks go up, and shareholders are happy. But what if you were the investor . . . what if you voted with your dollars by either refusing to do business with or invest in companies aligned to policies, ideologies, or initiatives that adversely impact the communities you want to support and instead put your dollars into companies that did champion the unique needs of your community swiftly, purposefully, and publicly?

This could change the way corporations think about supporting financial healing and equitable opportunities for employees, could reimagine profit sharing models, encourage investing in employee-owned business structures, or how they support community development financial institutions (CDFIs) that provide capital to underserved communities.

Companies can offer financial wellness programs that go beyond basic financial literacy workshops and address financial trauma, provide personalized coaching, and create safe spaces for employees to discuss financial challenges without stigma, all because of how you vote with your dollars. Of course, this won't be an individual effort, but an individual action can create a small ripple that leads to larger future ripples.

What About the Hardcore Capitalist?

Look, I've been dancing on the line in this book not to alienate my capitalism-leaning readers. Discussing community responsibility and condemning capitalism feels very . . . anti-American, doesn't it? What about personal agency and accountability? What about the free market?

Here's the truth no matter where you fall on the ideological spectrum: you can win big in capitalism. Start your own company. Scale it. Employ a small army. Become a high-powered exec with stock options and a seven-figure bonus. But even then, the odds are you don't own the infrastructure, tools, or systems your success depends on. Someone somewhere can turn it all off.

In fact, the only way capitalism truly "works" for individuals at scale is when others are being underpaid in relation to the profits generated, overworked, or excluded entirely, which is the entire premise of my thesis on financial trauma. And if you've made it this far in the book, you likely are someone who cares about trauma, equity, or healing, and you're not trying to get rich by exploiting people.

But you may still believe in capitalism—at least from the perspective of investing in business and generating profits. It's still assets over liabilities, but finding your values-based footing is important to this discussion because as we practice capitalism we have to embrace financial healing as a benefit to all. Investing in community well-being leads to a more stable economy and reduced crime and creates a more educated workforce. Yes, you can be critical of capitalism without being anti-capitalist, systems aware without being radical, and pro-reform without shouting "viva la revolucion!" Or you can take it all the way there, and that's entirely up to you.

Seven Ways to Practice Social Responsibility Now

1. Redirect autopilot giving. Replace default donations with vetted grassroots initiatives.
2. Start a giving circle. Pool funds monthly with friends or colleagues for collective giving.
3. Fund infrastructure, not just outcomes. Don't just pay for meals—pay the chefs a living wage.
4. Build or fund a community emergency fund. Give community members some financial cushion, not just advice.
5. Support trauma-informed educators. Fund speakers, writers, and organizers doing the healing work. If you can't fund them, make connections to those who can.
6. Mentor with purpose. Choose mentees from communities you care about.
7. Audit your investments. Are you profiting from companies doing harm? Change that ASAP.

Emotional Payoff

Giving aligned with your values regulates your nervous system. It affirms that your healing isn't selfish or that you aren't experiencing scarcity anymore. Your payoff (if you're looking for one) will exist in deeper community, renewed purpose, financial clarity, and legacy building.

Final Word

Financial healing is a collective journey. By embracing philanthropy and social responsibility, you can help to create systems that not only address financial trauma but also prevent it. It's time to move beyond performative acts of charity and toward meaningful reinvestment in our communities.

Ask yourself:

- What do I have to give?
- Who can I partner with?
- What would healing look like if it were shared?

If you possess the resources—be it time, money, or expertise—consider how you can contribute to this movement. Together, we can build a future where financial well-being is a right, not a privilege or an afterthought.

References

Anderson, C. (2001). *PowerNomics: The National Plan to Empower Black America*. Maryland: Powernomics Corp of America.

Bank of America (2024). 2024 Workplace Benefits Report survey. https://business.bofa.com/en-us/content/workplace-benefits/workplace-benefits-report-overview.html

DeGruy, J. (2005). *Post Traumatic Slave Syndrome: America's Legacy of Enduring Injury and Healing*. Uptone Press.

Durband, D. B., Law, R. H., & Mazzolini, A. K. (eds.) (2019). *Financial Counseling*. Springer.

Duhigg, C. (2014). *The Power of Habit*, New York: Random House.

FDIC (2023). National Survey of Unbanked and Underbanked Households. https://www.fdic.gov/household-survey/2023-fdic-national-survey-unbanked-and-underbanked-households-report

Felitti, V. J., Anda, R. F., Nordenberg, D., Williamson, D. F., Spitz, A. M., Edwards, V., Koss, M. P., & Marks, J. S. (1998). Relationship of childhood abuse and household dysfunction to many of the leading causes of death in adults: The Adverse Childhood Experiences (ACE) Study. *American Journal of Preventive Medicine,* 14(4), 245–258. https://doi.org/10.1016/S0749-3797(98)00017-8

Foster, S. (2024). Penny-pinching nation: More than a third of workers say they're living paycheck to paycheck. https://www.bankrate.com/credit-cards/news/living-paycheck-to-paycheck-statistics/#budget

Housel, M. (2020). *The Psychology of Money: Timeless Lessons on Wealth, Greed, and Happiness.* Harriman House.

HUD.gov. Attachment A—Section 8 Definition of Annual Income 24 CFR, Part 5, Subpart F (Section 5.609). https://www.hud.gov/sites/documents/calculatingattachment.pdf

Klontz, B. T., Britt, S. L., & Archuleta, K. L. (eds.). (2015), *Financial Therapy: Theory, Research, and Practice.* Springer.

Liebowitz, J. (ed.). (2018). *Financial Literacy Education: Addressing Student, Business, and Government Needs.* Florida: CRC Press.

Menakem, R. (2017). *My Grandmother's Hands: Racialized Trauma and the Pathway to Mending Our Hearts and Bodies.* Nevada: Central Recovery Press.

Sabree, R. (2023). "Ja Morant Demonstrates Another Side to Financial Trauma." https://rahkimsabree.substack.com/p/ja-morant-demonstrates-another-side

The Guardian (2005). Bank Admits It Owned Slaves. https://www.theguardian.com/world/2005/jan/22/usa.davidteather

University of Chicago (2020). Why a 19th century bank failure still matters. https://news.uchicago.edu/story/why-19th-century-bank-failure-still-matters

Van Der Kolk, B. (2015). *The Body Keeps the Score.* New York: Penguin.

Yehuda, R., & Lehrner, A. (2018). Intergenerational transmission of trauma effects: Putative role of epigenetic mechanisms. *World Psychiatry: Official Journal of the World Psychiatric Association (WPA),* 17 (3), 243–257. https://doi.org/10.1002/wps.20568

Whitebread, D., & Bingham, S. (2013). "Habit formation and learning in young children." London: Money Advice Service.

Acknowledgments

I want to acknowledge George Acheampong, who has been a mentor, advisor, big brother, and coach to me both professionally and personally. George has embarked on a mission to close the wealth gap by $100 billion through his company Melanin Money. He's been one of Investopedia's Top 100 Advisers in the nation for 2022 and 2023 and a Forbes contributor.

George, thank you for your friendship, mentorship, words of advice and encouragement, being available for my late-night brainstorming sessions, and the forever inspiration.

I also want to acknowledge my family, supporters, colleagues, and friends. Thank you for your encouragement, patience, and understanding during my absence while writing. Thank you for the reminder that this work is needed work.

Alberto, Steven, Alfonso, Aja, Travell, Mommie, thank you for being there in the trenches with me.

To the professional communities I'm a part of, The Financial Therapy Association, The Trauma of Money community, The Association for Financial Counseling, and Planning Education, thank you for being a point of reference, a professional home, and a resource before, during, and after the printing of this book. Thanks also to the Wiley team for believing in the timing and message that come with this work.

Dr. Joy DeGruy, Dr. Resmaa Menakem, Dr. Claud Anderson, Dr. Joe Dispenza, Dr. Brad Klontz, and countless others, thank you for your pioneering work that I've been able to absorb and build upon.

Last but certainly not least, I have to acknowledge my ancestors, starting with my grandfather, Baba Mwalimu r. Sabree I, whose presence I have felt with me the entirety of this project.

About the Author

Rahkim Sabree is an award-winning financial therapist, bestselling author, and sought-after speaker who helps individuals and organizations confront and heal from financial trauma. A leading voice at the intersection of race, mental health, identity, and money, Rahkim brings a deeply personal and culturally nuanced approach to financial wellness.

As the 2023 recipient of the Financial Therapy Association's Outstanding Community Outreach Leader Award, Rahkim has demonstrated a powerful commitment to financial empowerment through education, advocacy, and storytelling. In 2024, he earned AFCPE's Outstanding Consumer Financial Information Award for his Substack newsletter, where he unpacks the emotional and societal dimensions of money with raw honesty and insight.

Rahkim is also a two-time Plutus Award Winner (2023), recognized for excellence in financial media via his Substack, and was named a Top Innovative Coach by Business Insider in 2020. His work has been featured across many large publications, including The Grio, Black Enterprise, Forbes, Parents, Entrepreneur,

Business Insider, *The New York Times*, *The New York Post*, CNBC Make It!, Investopedia, Time, and more.

He is a frequent speaker for conferences, corporate audiences, nonprofits, and academic institutions across the country.

Rahkim's writing and workshops challenge conventional financial narratives by integrating his lived experiences with expertise in financial therapy, financial counseling, cultural commentary, and trauma responsive care. Whether guiding readers through his books or facilitating deep transformation in group and one-on-one settings, Rahkim's mission remains the same: to help people find empowerment, agency, and peace around money. Learn more at RahkimSabree.com.

Index

A

Access (creation), money (usage), 64
Accountability partners, 160
Action (TTM phase), 101
Adverse Childhood Experiences (ACEs), 17
Affirmations/rituals, rewiring tools,
    173–174, 177–178
American Dream, illusion, 57
Amygdala, threat perception, 76
Ancestral veneration, 178
Anderson, Claud, 83, 156–159
Anti-corporate identity, establish-
    ment, 67–68
Association for Financial Counseling and
    Planning Education (AFCPE)
    curriculum, 99
Attachment styles (financial boundary
    factor), 142

B

Banking
    services, 107
    system, trauma source, 117
Becoming Supernatural (Dispenza), 75, 131, 173

Bernays, Edward, 30
Bias, codification, 48
Black children, aspirations (limitation), 61
Black people, underclass, 47
Body
    engagement, exercise, 135
    financial trauma, manifestation, 73
    level, 132
    scams, 132, 148, 172, 177, 182
Body Keeps the Score, The (Van Der Kolk),
    76, 82, 153
Bottom-up regulation, 168–170, 177
Brainstem, 80
Breathwork, 164, 177, 182
Budgeting, healing mindset (usage), 119
Budgets
    adherence, difficulty, 31
    failures, 121
    problems, 120–122

C

Capitalism, 50–51, 54, 193–194
    Blacks/minorities (involvement), event
    footing (absence), 51

Capitalism (*Continued*)
  challenge, 152
  consumerism, impact, 62
  individualist values, 141
  navigation, 92
"Cash rules everything around me"
    (C.R.E.A.M.), 93
Chakras, 171
Chapman, Chantel, 142
Charity, 191–192
Chattel slavery, rationale, 36
Children (age 7), habit formation/
    learning, 86
Choice, illusion, 30–31
Christmas Carol, A (Dickens), 54
Class-based trauma, 93
Clean pain, 131
Code-switching, 40, 67
Collaborators, 160, 161
Collectivism, reclamation, 155–157
Communication strategies, practice, 144–145
Community
  building/focus, 56, 181, 182
  info sessions, organization, 160
  lending circles, usage, 156
  reinvestment, 191–192
  trauma recovery tool, 153–155
Community development financial
    institutions (CDFIs), 193
Conditioned compliance, 42–43
Consumerism, promotion, 61–62
Contemplation (TTM phase), 101
Corporate identity, destruction, 68
Corporate lingo, impact, 67
Corporate social responsibility, 192–193
Corporate structure, scarcity/competition
    (usage), 35
Counter transference, 114–115
Cultural clarity, absence, 63
Cultural discomfort, 58–59
Cultural engagement, 59
Cultural influences (financial boundary
    factor), 140
Cultural ripple, 64
Cultural taboos, 88

Culture, 183–184
  perspective, enlargement, 61
  weapon, 59–60

D

"Dear Money" exercise, 168
Deferred gratification, 53–56
DeGruy, Joy, 57, 61, 74, 79, 93–94
Dickens, Charles, 54
DiClemente, Carlo, 101
Dirty pain, 131
Dispenza, Joe, 75, 131, 173–174
Dopamine dependency, trigger, 30
Dress code, impact, 40–42, 67
Du Bois, W.E.B., 42
Duhigg, Charles, 30

E

Economic action steps, 158
Economic vampirism, 49
Employment
  opportunity, refusal, 68–69
  threats, 37
  trauma, 33, 51
Energy, activation, 38
Entrepreneurship, financial trauma, 64–70
Epigenetics, generational transfer
    (relationship), 81–83
Eurocentric white standards, contrast,
    45–46
Executives, interactions, 33–34
Expenses, elimination, 121–122
Exposure, Education, Execution (3 Es)
    (3E™ Framework), 1, 7–8, 71, 125,
    170, 179–181

F

Faith, issue, 53–56
Familial patterns (financial boundary
    factor), 140–141
Families
  abuse/hurt, 28
  dysfunction, 60
  emergency, response, 149
  expectations, 53

Fawn (trauma response), 78–79
Fear, 53–56, 153
  impacts, 21–22
  poverty/financial instability, impact, 31
Feelings/emotions, disentanglement, 37
Fight (trauma response), 78–79
Fight-or-flight response, 37, 152, 167
Financial abuse, power (relationship), 23–24
Financial advancement, practice, 92
Financial avoidance
  procrastination, comparison, 90
  understanding, 85
Financial benefits, engagement, 116–117
Financial boundaries
  absence, 63
  appearance, 146–147
  defining, 139–140
  establishment/setting, 59, 139
  factors, 140–143
  maintenance, 59
  reinforcement, 148–149
  setting, 62, 140, 148, 181
  survivor, remorse (relationship), 145–146
  understanding, 139–143
Financial decisions, money culture
    (impact), 60–61
Financial enmeshment, 141
Financial fawning, 39, 142
Financial fear
  client story, 15–17
  observation, usage, 15
Financial genogram, 172–173
Financial healing, 119, 123–124, 130, 174
  personal agency, possibility, 159
  practice, 175–178
Financial health, increase, 134
Financial identity, claim, 130–131
Financial instability, 25, 129
Financial institutions
  exclusion/exploitation, 47–48
  trust, rebuilding, 111–112
Financial invincibility, high income
    (relationship), 104–106
Financial knowledge, AFCPE definition, 99
Financial literacy, 181
  AFCPE definition, 99

anchor, 99–104
content, 74
intervention method, 97
Financially Irresponsible (Sabree), 74, 113
Financial narrative, 127–137
Financial planning, healing mindset (usage),
    119, 123–124
Financial privilege, armor, 48–49
Financial service providers, money
    shame, 86–87
Financial services, 107, 111–114, 183
Financial shame, understanding, 85
Financial socialization, 19–20
Financial stress, impact, 77
Financial support system, building,
    151, 160–161
Financial systems
  navigation, 103–104
  trust, rebuilding, 111–112
  willful nonparticipation, 109
Financial therapist, work title, 166
Financial therapy, 163–166, 176
Financial Therapy Association, xiv,
    75, 165, 201
*Financial Therapy: Theory, Research, and
    Practice* (Klontz), 166
Financial trauma, 3, 8–9, 35, 190
  generational trauma, impact, 74
  healing, steps, 127
  literacy, program (rooting), 180
  manifestation, 12–13, 73
  overcoming, 3Es, 1, 7, 71, 125
  reaction (survivor remorse), 146
  recognition, amygdala (usage), 77
  sources, 3
  understanding, 88, 109
  vicarious financial trauma, 17–18
Financial wellness program, building/
    implementation, 179, 183–185
First generational wealth builders,
    financial services usage,
    111–114
Flight (trauma response), 78–79
Forced financial compliance, 115
Freeze (trauma response), 78–79
Frontal lobe, function, 76

G

Generational money beliefs, 9–12
Generational transfer, epigenetics
    (relationship), 81–82
Generational trauma, epigenetics
    (impact), 51
Generational wealth building, promotion,
    49–50
Genogram, 172–173, 177
Group economics, 157–160

H

Habit
    building, 181
    formation/learning, 86
Healing, 163
    modalities, access (providing), 183
High income, financial invincibility
    (relationship), 104–106
Housel, Morgan, 103
Hughes, Steven M., 170–172
Human capital, 33, 35
Human cost, 33

I

Identity debt, 59–63
"I Fired My Boss" brand, 64–65
Indigenous/decolonized healing
    practices, 174–175
Individualism, 56–61, 152–153, 156, 182
Institutional financial trauma, 45
Institutional trauma, 93
Intergenerational racial trauma, 93
Interior ideals/low-bar standards,
    socialization, 61
Internal boundaries, 146–147
Internal champions, creation, 185
Isolation, identity (relationship), 67–70

J

Jim Crow, impact, 74
Job
    frustration, 36–37
    quitting, 38–39
JP Morgan Chase, public apology, 109–110

K

Klontz, Brad, 53–54, 91
Klontz Money Script® Inventory Revised
    (KMSI-R), 92–93, 133
Knowledge, spreading, 46

L

Life control, 59
Life trajectory, change, 38
Limbic system, 76, 80, 167
Long-term financial planning,
    conceptualization, 83

M

Maier, Steven, 79
Maintenance (TTM phase), 101
Mammalian brain (limbic system), 75
Managers, interactions, 33–34
Masterminds, creation, 160
Measurement metrics, 186–187
Mediocrity, acceptance, 102
Menakem, Resmaa, 159
Meritocracy, societal viewpoint, 57
Methylation patterns, passage, 82
Micro-habits, impact, 132
Milestone pressure, 59–63
Mind
    financial trauma, manifestation, 73
    level, 132
Mindfulness, 167–168, 182
Money
    avoidance, 89–92
    culture, impact, 60–61
    data, scheduling, 132
    discussion, counterintuition, 152
    evil, root, 53–54
    invincibility, 105–106
    map, 177
    memory, 99–100
    reaction, 82
    relationship, 60
    scripts, 91–96, 128
    shame, 85–89
    status, 91, 93–94
    story, 128

vigilance, 91, 94–95
worship, 91, 92–93
Mutual fund, investment, 112
My Grandmother's Hands (Menakem), 159

N
Narratives, shaping, 166
Neighborhood, poverty, 22–24
Neocortex, 75, 167
Nervous system, 75
  dysregulation, 111
  regulation (financial boundary factor),
    140, 142–143
Networking, 58
Neuroplasticity, 174
New financial self, embodiment
    (exercise), 136–137
Nonparticipation, 108–109
Norcross, John C., 101

O
Overcoming Financial Trauma™, 3E
    Model, 106

P
Panic, poverty/financial instability
    (impact), 31
Peer networks, 160–161
Personal financial management,
    frustrations, 62
Personal responsibility, path, 134
Philanthropy, 189
Polyvagal theory (Porges), 169
Pooled resources, usage, 156
Porges, Stephen, 169
Post Traumatic Slave Syndrome (DeGruy), 74
Post-traumatic stress disorder
    (PTSD), 87–88
Poverty, 22–25, 28–29, 51
Power, financial abuse (relationship), 23–24
PowerNomics (Anderson), 157–158
Power of Habit, The (Duhigg), 30
Precontemplation (TTM phase), 101
Predatory lending, 47–48
Prefrontal cortex, function, 76, 80

Preparation (TTM phase), 101
Prochaska, James O., 101
Professional guides, 160
Professionalism, praise, 41
Psychology of Money, The (Housel), 103
Public desires/fears/security/education,
    government/politician
    exploitation, 30–31

R
Race-based discrimination, immunity, 48
Racism, embeddedness/viewpoint, 47–48
Rakoff, Vivian, 82
Reconciliation, 110
Redlining, 47–48
Reiki, 166, 170–172, 177, 182, 183
Relational boundaries, 146, 147
Relationship, cultural strength, 57–58
Religion, leveraging, 55
Religious expectations, 53
Religious systems, money perceptions/
    interactions, 56
Reptilian (animal) brain, 75
Responsibility, distribution, 104–105
Retail therapy shame cycle, 88
Rich Dad, Poor Dad, 97
Robinhood, gamification
    investment, 30
Rollouts, staggering, 185

S
Safety, 34, 74–78
Saving
  healing mindset, usage, 119
  safety, 122–123
Second self, navigation, 39–42
Security
  absence, 153
  establishment/illusion, 34–35
  maintenance, 122
Seligman, Martin, 79
Shame, 89, 96, 153
Shame-based giving, 90
Situational boundaries, 146, 147
Slavery, Christianity justification, 55

SMART goals, establishment/setting, 143–144, 181
Social experiment, 41–42
Social mobility, increase, 64
Social responsibility, 189, 194
Societal expectations, 53
Somatic boundary awareness, 148
Somatic/emotional regulation work, prioritization, 182
Somatic healing, 164, 170–172, 177
Somatic movement, 164, 177
Soul level, 133–134
Sou-sous, participation, 157
Stress
    hormone regulation, 82–83
    observations (mice), 28
Stressors, body response, 31
Supervisors, interactions, 33–34
Supply/demand, education, 49
Survival, biology, 74–78
Survivor (remorse), financial boundaries (relationship), 145–146
Sympathetic nervous system (SNS), 168
Systemic financial trauma, 45

T
Thought patterns, rewiring (exercise), 134
Three-part financial boundary setting framework, 143–145
Top-down regulation (grounding), 167–168, 176, 182
transference, 114–115
Transtheoretical Model of Change (TTM), phases, 101–102
Trauma
    bonds, creation, 29
    company culture, impact, 34
    financial boundary factor, 140, 142
    increase, 89
    inflicting/perpetuating, 110
    isolation, 154–155
    response(s), 65–67, 69, 78–79
    viewpoint/question, 63

Trauma-bonded relationship, 58
Trauma-informed perspectives/ approach, 115, 121
Trauma of Money, The, 39
Trauma responsive perspectives/ approach, 115, 121
Triune brain model/framework, 76–77, 80
TRUST™ Framework, development, 117–118
Trust, rebuilding, 111–112, 114–118

U
United States, capitalism-driven economy, 35

V
Vacant esteem, 94
Vagus nerve, 168–170
Values, auditing, 143
Van Der Kolk, Bessel, 76, 153–155, 167
Vendors, 160, 161
Vicarious financial trauma, 17–18, 51
Vicarious trauma, 15–17, 88
Visibility pipelines, creation, 160

W
Wealth accumulation, fear (education), 55
Wealth building, 49–50, 55
White supremacy system, Black people (relationship), 47
White voice, 40
Willful nonparticipation, ignorance (contrast), 108–109
Workplace
    chattel slavery, rationale, 36
    toxicity, 39
    trauma, 33, 51, 88
Wretched state, 29

Y
Yehuda, Rachel, 82